IMAGES
of America

Remembering
GEORGIA'S
CONFEDERATES

Surrounding the Great Seal of Georgia of 1861 are six men who shaped Georgia's Confederate future. U.S. senator Robert Toombs became the Confederate secretary of state, resigned to become a brigadier general, and was one of Georgia's greatest orators. U.S. representative Alexander H. Stephens became vice president of the Confederacy, was imprisoned for a short time after the war, later became a U.S. senator and Georgia's governor, and died in office. Hershel V. Johnson, a former Georgia governor and U.S. senator, was the running mate for Stephen A. Douglas in the 1860 election against Abraham Lincoln; he served as a Confederate senator and was elected U.S. senator but not allowed to serve. Benjamin Harvey Hill, a powerful state legislator, was a Confederate senator and, after the war, a leading U.S. senator. Howell Cobb was a U.S. Speaker of the House, governor, and U.S. secretary of the treasury under President Buchanan; he acted as president of the Secession Convention and served as a brigadier general in the war. Joseph E. Brown was Georgia's only Confederate governor, and his disputes with Jefferson Davis were legendary; he later became a U.S. senator from Georgia. Georgia's Secession Convention met on January 16, 1861, to decide the issue. Stephens, Johnson, and Hill opposed secession with Toombs and Cobb supporting. After the vote was cast on January 19, 1861, all followed the majority, and Georgia declared itself a free and independent republic. Georgia's counties Ben Hill, Johnson, Stephens, and Toombs are named for these leaders. (*History of Georgia*, 1898.)

IMAGES
of America

Remembering
GEORGIA'S
CONFEDERATES

Dr. David N. Wiggins

Published by Arcadia Publishing
Charleston SC, Chicago IL, Portsmouth NH, San Francisco CA

Printed in Great Britain

Library of Congress Catalog Card Number: 2005923149

For all general information contact Arcadia Publishing at:
Telephone 843-853-2070
Fax 843-853-0044
E-mail sales@arcadiapublishing.com
For customer service and orders:
Toll-Free 1-888-313-2665

Visit us on the internet at http://www.arcadiapublishing.com

Today we continue to honor the memory of those Georgians who served her as a part of the Confederate States of America. Pictured here at one such example of how we remember veterans today are members of the award-winning Forrest's Escort SCV [Sons of Confederate Veterans] Camp's Honor Guard. Those pictured are L. A. Burns, Gene Moore, Roger Denney, Robby Robison, Rick Pope, Ed Daniell, and Tony Gonzalez. This book is dedicated to the men and women who served Confederate Georgia and to those who remember them. Lest we forget! (Courtesy of Forrest's Escort Camp #1239 SCV and Cmdr. Charlie Lott.)

CONTENTS

ACKNOWLEDGMENTS

This project began as a work about vintage images of Georgia's Confederate monuments and memorials; however, due to overwhelming support from contributors, it became something quite different than planned. The book became the story of the men and women themselves, such that the idea behind the original book must be told at a later date.

This work features a large number of images from contributors from all over the state, and to all, the author extends his thanks and gratitude. Three gentlemen in particular—John W. Lynch, Sam Pyle, and David W. Vaughn—greatly enhanced the work with their personal collections, special knowledge, and willingness to share. Their additional assistance with caption material was invaluable, and new friendships have been made.

The author would be remiss in not mentioning a few other main contributors: SCV Georgia Division commander Jack Bridwell, executive director of the Museum of Colquitt County; Reagan Grimsley of Columbus State University; Tina Harris of Jackson County Historical Society; Ann R. Harrison and the staff of Thomas County Historical Society; Kaye Lanning Minchew and the staff of Troup County Archives; Scott B. Thompson Sr., director of Dublin-Laurens Museum; Cmdr. Charlie Lott; Mike Couch; Jerry A. Maddox; Susan Patton Hamersky; and Dr. Roy Ward.

Information was gathered from a variety of sources, including the internet. Two Georgia authors and their works were inspiring to the author and were great resources: Frank McKenney's *The Standing Army* and Robert Kerlin's *Confederate Generals of Georgia and Their Burial Sites* should be owned by every Georgia Confederate researcher. Additional resources and recommended reading can be found at the end of the work.

Institutional archivists and their staffs across the state were most helpful, as were many individual contributors not named above. I only wish there was enough room to name all; however, to all of you I say thank you for allowing this dream to become a reality. The source of each image is indicated at the end of the caption where appropriate, and when none is given, it is in the author's personal collection. Any mistake or omission in these credits was unintended.

My sincerest thanks are extended to Arcadia Publishing for their support in this project, with a special thanks to Ms. Laura New, production coordinator, whose guidance and encouragement will always be appreciated. Special thanks is also extended to my wife, Sara, and my family for their understanding and support. The author also wishes to thank all those countless unnamed individuals who gave directions or told me where to go, and a special thanks to those that didn't!

INTRODUCTION

"Lest we forget!," a sentiment that can be found on monuments throughout the South, represents the thoughts behind the work *Remembering Georgia's Confederates*. The work is dedicated to the Georgians, both men and women, who served her at a time when her heart belonged to another country, the Confederate States of America. The work presented here is about remembering Georgia's Confederate past, a time of passion, devotion, honor, courage, faith, perseverance, sacrifice, and loss. The work is not meant as a glorification of war, but as a remembrance to those Georgians who believed in their state and were willing to give their all—our heritage. Over 125,000 Georgians fought for the Confederacy, with over 25,000 giving their lives in defense of the state.

Included within the pages of this volume are vintage images of some of Georgia's most famous and lesser-known citizens who served her in war, as well as images of young and old who went off to war, many never to return. The work features Georgia's proclaimed youngest veteran as well as the Confederacy's oldest general. Georgians served with distinction in the infantry, cavalry, artillery, navy, marines, medical, and quartermaster departments, as well as the Confederate government. This collection of images gives the viewer the opportunity to see the wide variety of uniforms and weapons that Georgians had at their disposal. It also gives the reader the opportunity to learn of the bravery of some of its lesser-known citizens like Virgil Brown, Thomas Overby, and Patrick Wier.

Those fortunate enough to have survived the war found a devastated land and economy at their feet, but Georgians rebuilt, and those left behind remembered their fallen comrades. Images of men who served together are featured in the book in the form of celebrations at memorial services, parades, reunions, and dedications. Georgia hosted four national Confederate reunions, and the one in Macon in 1912 is featured in the work with a number of rare images. The thin gray line got thinner until there was but one in Georgia, whose image is featured.

Also featured in this work are a few of the monuments of stone and bronze found within the state that were dedicated in honor of Confederate individuals, both Georgians and non-Georgians. These individuals included Jefferson Davis, N. B. Forrest, Thomas J. "Stonewall" Jackson, Joseph E. Johnston, Robert E. Lee, and Leonidas Polk. Georgia has over 140 county monuments to their honored dead, and hopefully, they will be featured in a future work by the author.

Georgia is rich in its heritage, and there are numerous places that one can visit to learn about and remember its Confederate past. A few of these sites are featured in the work, but many more can be found across the state. The battlefields of Chickamauga, Kennesaw, and Pickett's Mill all have wonderful interpretive centers. The world's largest painting, *The Battle of Atlanta*, can be seen at the Cyclorama, along with the engine *Texas*. The Southern Museum of Civil War and Locomotive History in Kennesaw houses the *General*. The DuBose Collection at the Atlanta

History Center features one of the finest collections of Confederate artifacts in the state. Rhodes Hall in Atlanta features one of the most unique memorials, the Rise and Fall of the Confederacy, in stained glass, and the world's largest Confederate memorial is on display at Stone Mountain. The forts of Pulaski, McAllister, and Jackson show Confederate coastal defenses, and for naval history, Port Columbus National Naval Museum is beyond its peers. Fort Tyler at West Point was the last fort to fall and saw the end of the war in Georgia. Washington, Georgia, had the last Confederate cabinet meeting. In Irwinville, President Jefferson was captured, and today it is the site of the Jefferson Davis Historical Site. Confederate cemeteries dot the state and are well worth visiting; a few are Cassville, Dalton, Kingston, Laurel Grove in Savannah, Marietta, Magnolia in Augusta, Myrtle Hill in Rome, Oakland in Atlanta, Rose Hill in Macon, and Resaca.

Smaller museums across the state offer many artifacts and should be explored. A few include the A. H. Stephens Museum in Crawfordville, Bartow History Center in Cartersville, Male Museum in Newnan, Blue-Gray Museum in Fitzgerald, Little Drummer Boy Museum in Andersonville, Marietta Museum in the old Kennesaw House in Marietta, Rome Area Museum, and Thomas County Museum in Thomasville. The homes of many leaders like Hill, Stephens, and Toombs are available to visit. For remembering prisoners of war, Andersonville must be visited.

In a work like this that is so broad, you can never include everything that you would like; there are always more soldiers, more sites, and more reunion shots. The author has made an effort to include all areas of the state. Georgia is a very large state and has hundreds of sites to visit, and any mistakes or omissions are not intentional. The author's objective was to publish an accurate and factual overview of some Georgians who served. If you wish to express comments, questions concerning book orders, or requests for signed copies, or if you have images you would like to share or be considered for possible future works, please contact the author at remgaconfed@aol.com or write him at 1093 Oak Grove Road, Carrollton, Georgia 30117.

This old engraved image shows Georgia troops rallying at the First Battle of Manassas on July 21, 1861. Note the flag with state seal. During the battle, Col. Francis S. Bartow from Savannah was leading a brigade when he charged and was mortally wounded. Dying in Colonel Gartrell's arm, he reportedly said, "They have killed me boys, but never give up the fight." General Bartow's remains were returned to Georgia, and he is buried in Savannah's Laurel Grove Cemetery; see page 111. (*The Century War Book*, 1888.)

One

GEORGIANS WENT TO WAR

This rare photograph shows Georgia troops training at Camp Stephens in Griffin, Georgia, in the early 1860s. The camp was located a half mile east of the railroad and two miles north of Griffin. Many units trained at this camp, and close inspection shows four squads dressed in different uniforms on the field. Spectators can be seen around the area watching the men at work. Note the ladies' parasols and the buggies. (*Confederate Stamps, Old Letters, and History.*)

Known as "Old Davy," "The Horse," and "Bengal Tiger," David Emanuel Twiggs was born in Richmond County in 1790. He served as a major in the War of 1812 and the Seminole and Black Hawk Indian Wars. In 1836, he was a colonel of dragoons in the Mexican War. He was brevetted brigadier and then major general. In 1861, he was the second ranking officer in the U.S. Army. Upon secession, he was immediately appointed major general in the Confederate Army and was the oldest ranking member. He was assigned the command of the district of Louisiana. He died in 1862 and is buried in Augusta. (Courtesy of Library of Congress.)

"Old Reliable," Gen. William Joseph Hardee, was born in Camden County, Georgia. Graduating from West Point in 1838, he was twice brevetted for gallantry during the Mexican War. He wrote *Rifle and Light Infantry Tactics*, the main manual for the U.S. Army. The Hardee hat was named in his honor. Resigning his commission when Georgia seceded, he organized the Arkansas "Hardee's Brigade." Recognized as the top corps commander of the Army of Tennessee, he fought at Shiloh, Perryville, Murfreesboro, Missionary Ridge, and Atlanta and later headed the military department of South Carolina, Georgia, and Florida. He died in 1873 and is buried at Live Oak Cemetery in Selma, Alabama.

This image of an unidentified Confederate drummer is characteristic of the young who went off to war. It is from a Macon estate and shows the young drummer wearing a kepi and holding his drum with a sling around his neck. The image is probably from early in the war, since the individual soldier or unit often decorated the drums with patriotic drawings or words. (Courtesy of David W. Vaughan.)

Sixty-one members of Company D, "Oglethorpe Infantry," Ramsey's 1st Georgia Infantry, are shown standing on the parade grounds on March 16, 1861. This regiment is reportedly the first to have left the state. They served in Florida until they were transferred to western Virginia to serve under Robert E. Lee and Stonewall Jackson. Mustered out in March 1862, the men organized as Company B, 12th Georgia Artillery Battalion. Serving for a while in eastern Tennessee and then the coast of Georgia, the company then became part of the Army of Tennessee under Johnston and then Hood in the defense of Georgia. The image is believed to have been taken in Augusta. (Review of Reviews Company, 1911.)

William S. Askew enlisted as a private in Company A, "Newnan Guards," Ramsey's 1st Georgia Infantry, on May 7, 1861. He was discharged on August 21, 1861. He enlisted as a private in Company F, 16th Battalion Georgia Cavalry, on May 2, 1862. Captured at Knoxville, Tennessee, in 1863, he was sent to Camp Morton, Indiana. He transferred to Company F, 13th Regiment Georgia Cavalry, on May 2, 1864, where he was appointed fourth corporal. He was then transferred from Camp Morton, Indiana, to Fort Delaware, Delaware, and paroled there in February 1865. He died in Newnan in April 1917. (Courtesy of Library of Congress.)

William McD. Felder enlisted as a private on March 18, 1861, in Houston County in Company C, "Southern Rights Guards," Ramsey's 1st Georgia Infantry. Early in the war, he saw action in the West Virginia and Shenandoah Valley campaigns. The regiment mustered out of service in March of 1862. Soon afterwards, he enlisted in the Georgia State Troops and served as a private for the remainder of the war with Company G, 8th Regiment, Third Brigade, Georgia Militia. He is photographed wearing a gray, nine-button frock coat, slouch hat, and belt with the Georgia seal, and he has a lit cigar in his hand. (Courtesy of David W. Vaughan.)

John L. Ells of Augusta enlisted as first sergeant in Company G, "Confederate Light Guards," 3rd Georgia Infantry, on April 26, 1861. He was elected second lieutenant on June 19, 1862. He was wounded at the Battle of Sharpsburg on September 17, 1862, and was wounded again at Manassas Gap on July 23, 1863, when a bullet lodged near his right hip joint. He was forced to retire from service. He wears a double-breasted jacket with two rows of seven buttons, and the single bar on his collar indicates his rank. (Courtesy of David W. Vaughan.)

George S. Sharp was born on April 29, 1818, and served first as captain of Company F, 3rd Regiment Georgia State Troops, and later as captain of Company I, 7th Regiment Georgia, State Guards Infantry. The 1860 census shows him living in Carroll County with his wife and three children. He was the son of an early Carroll settler, Hiram Sharp, and the area known as Sharp Creek is named for him. Having died on April 17, 1903, he is buried in the Sharp Cemetery in Carroll County. He is posed in a regular seven-button jacket and pinned back slouch hat and carries a curved cavalry saber. (Courtesy of Sam Pyle and McDaniel-Curtis SCV Camp.)

Richard A. Ford, son of Rev. John and Jane Ford in Rutherford County, North Carolina, was born on October 15, 1819. Richard enlisted in Company E, 3rd Battalion, Georgia Infantry, and poses with a kepi that has the letters "H G," for "Holloway Grays," from Upson County, Georgia. He died March 30, 1863, in Shelbyville, Tennessee, and is buried in the Confederate section of Willow Mount Cemetery in Shelbyville. He had three sons who served in Georgia units. On May 6, 1863, the 3rd and 9th Battalions of Georgia Infantry consolidated to form the 37th Georgia. (Courtesy of Billie Tatom Ford, widow of Orval W. Ford, great-grandson of Richard.)

This image was discovered in a trunk in a Cartersville estate that also contained memorabilia associated with the 4th Georgia Infantry. The 4th Georgia consisted of troops from Talbot, Troup, Twiggs, Dougherty, Gordon, Jasper, Baldwin, Macon, and Sumter Counties. This unidentified private poses with a conversion musket and massive fighting knife. He wears a red-and-white Corsican cap trimmed with lace, his dark uniform has seven large buttons showing, and his uniform is adorned with a red sash. (Courtesy of David W. Vaughan.)

Jeremiah "Jerry" Brown Morgan enlisted as a second lieutenant in Company B, "LaGrange Light Guards," 4th Georgia Infantry, on April 26, 1861. On October 4, 1861, he was appointed commissary officer for the regiment. He resigned seven days later to take the same position for Colquitt's Brigade. He remained in service until the end of the war and surrendered in Greensboro, North Carolina, on April 26, 1865. He died in Atlanta on June 24, 1884, and is buried in Hillview Cemetery in Griffin. He poses in his dark "L L G" uniform, shako hat with feathered plume to his side, holding a ceremonial sword. (Courtesy of Troup County Archives.)

Miles H. Hill enlisted as a first lieutenant in Company B, LaGrange Light Guards, 4th Georgia Infantry, on April 26, 1861. He was elected captain on May 8, 1862. His younger brother Joe Hill served as a sergeant in the company. Sergeant Hill was killed by a cannon ball during the Battle of Fredericksburg, dying on December 16, 1862. Captain Hill wrote home, "His death is very much lamented by the company as his kind and generous manners drew all hearts to him." Captain Hill resigned almost three weeks later on January 6, 1863, and died in Valdosta in 1870. (Courtesy of Troup County Archives.)

Palmon Ernest Ferrell enlisted as a private on June 21, 1861, in Company D, "West Point Guards," 4th Georgia Infantry. He died of malaria at a hospital in Portsmouth, Virginia, on September 30, 1861. His body was returned to Georgia and is buried in Hillview Cemetery in LaGrange. Here, he poses in matching light-colored pants and jacket featuring a black collar and black shoulder straps. His double-buckled belt appears to have "slim jim" hand-stitched holsters. He wears a black slouch hat and is armed with a pair of revolvers and a musket with bayonet. (Courtesy of Troup County Archives.)

Pvt. James J. McKinley lived in Baldwin County when he enlisted into Company H, "Baldwin Blues," 4th Georgia Infantry. He served with the unit until June 18, 1864, when he was detailed to the quartermaster's department in Georgia. He died of yellow fever in Savannah in 1875 and is reportedly buried there. Note the *carte de visite* was addressed to his parents, "Your Son, J. J. McK." The 4th Georgia served as part of the Doles-Cook Brigade and surrendered with the Army of Northern Virginia. (Courtesy of David W. Vaughan.)

Soldiers of Company K, "Sumter Light Guards" of Sumter County, 4th Georgia Infantry, are pictured on parade grounds. The regiment left Americus, Georgia, on April 27, 1861, and mustered in May in Augusta, where this image was likely taken. The building in the background appears to be the same as in the image of the 1st Georgia on page 11. The regiment saw action at Seven Pines, Chancellorsville, Gettysburg, and the Appomattox Campaign. The regiment was a part of the famous Cook-Doles Brigade, named after two Georgia generals.

Recruits of Company A, "Clinch Rifles," 5th Georgia Infantry, pose in front of an open tent in camp at Macon on May 10, 1861, the day before the company was mustered into service. The men appear to be relaxed and confident of their purpose, mission, and outcome. The early uniforms and hats of the Clinch Rifles were dark green. The initials C. R. can be seen above the tent and on the washtub. The 1841 rifles and sword bayonets are stacked to the right. (Courtesy of U.S. Army Military History Institute.)

Officers and non-commissioned officers (NCOs) of the Clinch Rifles, which later became Company A, 5th Georgia Infantry, pose in front of an open tent *c.* 1861. The 5th saw major action at Murfreesboro. At Chickamauga, over 55 percent of the regiment was killed or wounded. The original captain was Charles A. Platt, who left due to age. First Lt. David Henry Ansley became captain but was wounded and permanently disabled at Missionary Ridge. Note the reversed "C. R." above the tent opening. (Courtesy of U.S. Army Military History Institute.)

Thomas Patrick Wier was born in Georgia on May 26, 1839. He enlisted as a private in Company B, "Griffin Light Guards," 5th Georgia Infantry, on May 10, 1861. He was wounded on September 19, 1863, at the Battle of Chickamauga, and listed as wounded again in a Confederate hospital on December 30, 1864. Picked by comrades-in-arms, he was placed on the Confederate Roll of Honor for his "display of courage and devotion on the field of battle" at Chickamauga. He died on April 6, 1908. (Courtesy of John W. Lynch.)

On May 11, 1861, Albertus T. Guice was made first corporal of Company G, 5th Georgia Infantry. Company G came from Schley County. Later appointed sergeant major, he was killed at the Battle of Resaca at Tanner's Ferry, Georgia, on May 15, 1864. The 5th had major losses at Chickamauga. This early image shows him in an ornate coat with three rows of buttons, a dark collar, and sergeant stripes. Armed with a sword and revolver, he wears a shako hat with two brass emblems and a short circular pompon. (Courtesy of Rome Area History Museum.)

William Lewis Salisbury joined the 5th Georgia Infantry in the Army of Northern Virginia as a major on May 10, 1861. He retired at reorganization on May 8, 1862. He returned to Georgia and raised the 5th Infantry Regiment, Georgia State Guard, becoming Colonel Salisbury. His kepi has the letters "G G" for "Georgia Grays," Company I of the 5th Georgia from Muscogee County. After the war, he owned the Columbus newspaper the *Enquirer Sun*. In a feud over an alleged libelous remark with Dr. R. U. Palmer, he was murdered on April 21, 1878, in Phoenix City, Alabama. (Courtesy of David W. Vaughan.)

Pvt. James D. Means joined the "Ordnance Guard" in 1863, which became Company A, 5th Regiment, Georgia Reserves. The 5th Reserve Force was responsible for guarding Union prisoners at Camp Oglethorpe near Macon. On July 30, 1864, the reserves were called into service and successfully defended Macon from Sherman's forces. Soon thereafter, Private Means developed typhoid fever and died at his Houston County home on November 19, 1864. He is wearing a dark frock coat, gray forage cap, leather waist belt with frame buckle, "Augusta style" cap box, and shoulder strap that likely supports a haversack. (Courtesy of David W. Vaughan.)

Alfred Holt Colquitt was born in Monroe, Georgia, on April 20, 1824. Graduating from Princeton, he was admitted to the Bar in 1845. He served as a major in the Mexican War, the U.S. Congress, and the Georgia Senate. Commissioned as a colonel in the 6th Georgia, he became brigadier general on September 1, 1862. The brigade fought battles at Fredericksburg, Chancellorsville, and Olustee. He surrendered with his brigade in Greensboro on April 26, 1865. He served as Georgia governor from 1877 to 1882 and as U.S. senator from 1883 to 1894, when he died in office. He is buried at Rose Hill Cemetery in Macon. (Courtesy of State of Florida Archives.)

Joseph W. Parks enlisted as a private in Company A, "Coweta Guards," 7th Georgia Infantry, on July 30, 1861. Wounded at Malvern Hill, Virginia, he died from the wounds at Richmond, Virginia, on July 11, 1862. Note the Italian-style hat he is wearing. Two other Parks served in this company: Albertus Parks, killed near Yorktown, and 1st Lt. Thomas B. Park. The regiment's first engagement was at the First Battle of Manassas, part of Francis Bartow's Brigade. General Bartow was killed and, from the official report, "the promising life of Bartow, while leading the Seventh Georgia Regiment, was quenched in blood." (Courtesy of Male Academy Museum of Newnan-Coweta.)

On the wall of the Male Academy Museum in Newnan is a portrait of William Thomas Overby next to his Confederate Medal of Honor. Often called the "Nathan Hale of the Confederacy," he grew up in Coweta County; joined Company A, 7th Georgia Infantry; and was wounded at the Second Battle of Manassas in 1862. After working as a nurse, he joined Mosby's Rangers and was captured at Fort Royal, Virginia, on September 23, 1864. Refusing to give the location of Mosby in exchange for his life, he was hung without trial from a walnut tree. Buried at Fort Royal, his body was returned to Newnan to much fanfare in January 1998. (Courtesy of Male Academy Museum of Newnan-Coweta.)

William Robert Whatley, born on August 22, 1810, lived most of his life in Fayette County. He enlisted in Company D, 7th Georgia State Militia. In 1863, he enrolled in Company C, 4th Georgia State Militia, and was commissioned as a fourth lieutenant in 1864. Records indicate he was an escort to General Hood in September 1864. Wounded at the Battle of Griswoldville, Georgia, in the mouth and left foot, he survived the war and served in the Georgia legislature and as postmaster of Fayetteville. He died on July 21, 1910, a month prior to his 100th birthday. (Courtesy of John W. Lynch, great-great-grandson of William.)

Branch brothers John L., Hamilton M., and Sanford W. entered service with Company B, "Oglethorpe Light Infantry," 8th Georgia Infantry. John graduated from Georgia Military Institute; was second lieutenant, first lieutenant, and adjutant for Francis Bartow; and was killed at First Manassas on July 21, 1861. Hamilton was commissioned a lieutenant in the 54th Georgia in 1862 and was severely wounded in defense of Atlanta. Sanford was captured at First Manassas, paroled, severely wounded at Gettysburg, and captured, and he became one of the Immortal 600 (see page 94). Mauriel Phillips Joslyn's *Charlotte's Boys* features war letters of the Branch family. Many artifacts of the brothers are on display at the Atlanta History Center. (Courtesy of Kenan Research Center at the Atlanta History Center.)

James Henry Harrison Brown was born on March 15, 1841, in Oglethorpe County, Georgia. He enlisted as a private in Company K, "Oglethorpe Rifles," 8th Georgia Infantry. He was wounded at the Seven Days' Battles in 1862 and again at Petersburg near the end of the war. He surrendered at Appomattox, Virginia, on April 9, 1865, and died on November 16, 1923. He is posed in a darker jacket and matching pants with a pinned slouch hat. He holds his percussion musket, and the long tongue cap pouch on his belt is like the ones produced by the Augusta Arsenal. (Courtesy of John Britton Wells III.)

First Cpl. William Green Gaithers Raines volunteered to serve with Company C, "Hillyers' Rifles" of Walton County, 9th Georgia Infantry, on June 13, 1861. The 9th Georgia was assigned to Anderson's Brigade in the Army of Northern Virginia except when assigned to General Longstreet in the Suffolk campaign and at Knoxville. Raines was wounded at Gettysburg, where the 9th saw major action, and was killed in action at Knoxville on December 18, 1863. He is seen here in a typical seven-button frock coat. (Courtesy of David W. Vaughan.)

Leander Jack Green was born in Bulloch County, Georgia, in October 1836. A member of Company H, "Brooks County Rifles," 9th Georgia Infantry, he was wounded by gunshot in his left arm at the Battle of Fredericksburg. This image was taken after the battle, and swelling is visible in his left hand. While on leave, he was used by the county to take food and provisions to needy families of men still fighting. After the war, he moved to Florida with his family and died July 17, 1916. (Courtesy of S. Martin Barker, great-great-grandson of Leander.)

John L. Blalock was born on July 25, 1832. He was first elected as a junior second lieutenant of Company I, "Fayette Grey Guards," 10th Georgia Infantry, in May 1861 but resigned due to disability in December 1861. He was later elected second lieutenant of Company G, "Huie Guards," 44th Georgia Infantry, on March 4, 1862, and captain on December 4, 1864. He contracted and died of tuberculosis in a Charlottesville, Virginia, hospital on March 30, 1863. His body was returned home to Fayette County and was interred in the Blalock family cemetery southwest of Fayetteville. (Courtesy of Fayette County Historical Society.)

John James Fillyaw enlisted as a private in March 1862 at Isabella, Worth County, in Company B, "Worth Rebels," 10th Battalion Georgia Infantry. The initial formation of the regiment was in Americus, Georgia, during the spring of 1862. The 10th Battalion of Georgia Volunteers was listed as assigned to Military District of Georgia, commanded by Brig. Gen. Hugh W. Mercer. On December 15, 1862, the 10th was ordered to proceed to Virginia to join Robert E. Lee's Army of Northern Virginia. Private Fillyaw surrendered at Appomattox Courthouse. Here, he is armed with a D-Guard Bowie knife and musket with bayonet. (Courtesy of Museum of Colquitt County History, Jack Bridwell, executive director.)

James McEachern, born in Georgia on July 26, 1840, enlisted in Company I, Fayette Grey Guards, 10th Georgia Infantry, on May 27, 1861. Wounded at the Battle of Gettysburg on July 2, 1863, he surrendered at Appomattox. He died on January 17, 1893, and is buried at the Fayetteville City Cemetery. Two brothers served in the same unit; Daniel was killed in the Seven Days' Battles, and Pleasant Marion surrendered with James. Images of his brothers in their uniforms and additional information can be found in *The Dorman-Marshborune Letters* by John W. Lynch. (Courtesy of John W. Lynch.)

William Parks Redwine was born in Campbell County in 1826. He enlisted as second lieutenant of Company I, "Fayette Rifle Grays," 10th Georgia Infantry. He was then elected first lieutenant on February 3, 1862, and captain on September 14, 1862. After resigning on July 18, 1864, he returned home to Fayetteville. After the war, he became its first mayor and served in the Georgia General Assembly and as a commissioner of roads. He married Mary Grace Trimble, and they had nine children. He died in 1890 and is buried in the Fayetteville City Cemetery. (Courtesy of Fayette County Historical Society and John W. Lynch.)

First Lt. Russell Glenn Stickland, born in May 1838, enlisted in Company I, Fayette Rifle Grays, 10th Georgia Infantry, on May 27, 1861. He was appointed adjutant on December 31, 1861. A superb marksman, he often led the regiment's sharpshooters. During the Battle of Knoxville in November 1863, he was cited for "gallantry and good conduct" by Gen. LaFayette McLaws. Strickland was wounded in the Battle of Cold Harbor, Virginia, on June 3, 1864, and was sent to Richmond's Jackson Hospital, where he died on June 14, 1864. (Courtesy of John W. Lynch and Fayette County Historical Society.)

The son of Rev. Thomas and Emily Wood of Walton County, Thomas G. Wood was orphaned by age 16 in 1860 and lived in a Social Circle, Georgia, boarding home with his teacher. He joined Company H, "Walton Infantry," 11th Georgia Infantry, and was the regiment's "pet and idol." The 11th was mustered on July 3, 1861, and soon boarded trains for Virginia. That fall, Wood developed pneumonia, went to a Richmond hospital, and died on December 13, 1861. He is buried in Richmond's Oakwood Cemetery. Note his initials in the bill of his kepi. (Courtesy of David W. Vaughan.)

Brothers John A. and James L. Teague of Gilmer County are posed for this family photograph. John was born in 1830 and first joined Company I, 1st Georgia Regulars, Army of Tennessee, in 1861. He was wounded at Yorktown in 1862; became a lieutenant in Company C, 30th Battalion, 11th Georgia Cavalry; and was dischargd in Charleston, South Carolina, in 1865. James served as a private in Company D, 11th Georgia Infantry; was captured at Gettysburg on July 3, 1863; and died of typhoid on October 29, 1863. He is buried at Fort Delaware, Maryland. (Courtesy of Charles W. Teague.)

Pvt. G. R. Barrett enlisted on March 4, 1862, in Company A, "Gainesville Light Infantry," 11th Georgia Infantry. The 11th was present at the Siege of Yorktown, Seven Days' Battles, Campaign in Northern Virginia, Sharpsburg or Antietam, Fredericksburg, Gettysburg, Chickamauga, Chattanooga-Ringold, Richmond Campaign, and Appomattox, where the unit surrendered with the Army of Northern Virginia. He appears to be wearing a forage hat with havelock, coat with dark collar, and a large D-Guard Bowie knife. (Courtesy of Sam Pyle and McDaniel-Curtis SCV Camp.)

Samuel R. Rentz was born in Echols County on February 22, 1839. He enlisted as a private on June 14, 1861, with Company I, "Lowndes Volunteers," 12th Georgia Infantry. He was captured at Front Royal, Virginia, on May 30, 1862, and was exchanged in August 1862. Captured at Spotsylvania on May 10, 1864, he was released at Elmira, New York, on June 21, 1864. He died on November 29, 1915, and is buried at Oakdale Church Cemetery in Colquitt County. (Courtesy of Museum of Colquitt County History, Jack Bridwell, executive director.)

Habersham Clayton Towns (left) and Henry Harrison Towns joined Company K, "Evans Guards" of Troup County, 13th Georgia Infantry, on July 3, 1861. The 13th was mustered into service on July 8, 1861, at Griffin and served with Floyd's Brigade in West Virginia. Reassigned to Lawton's Brigade, later Lawton-Gordon-Evans Georgia Brigade, the 13th served with distinction in the Seven Days' Battles and served with the Army of Northern Virginia until surrendering. Both men surrendered at Appomattox; they are posed here with large D-Guard Bowie knives. Their uniforms differ slightly at the shoulders and collar. (Courtesy of Troup County Archives.)

Shirley Nathaniel Sledge (left) and Robert Hill Sledge Jr. were privates in Company K, "Evans Guards," 13th Georgia Infantry. Shirley was detached and elected as captain of Company H, 2nd Regiment Georgia Cavalry State Guards, on August 9, 1863. He mustered out on January 31, 1864, and returned to Company K that same year. Robert was permanently disabled at Gettysburg on July 2, 1863, and was discharged. Three other Sledge boys served in the unit: John W., who lost an arm in prison; M. M., who was captured at Cedar Creek, Virginia, in 1865; and Nathan H. (Courtesy of Troup County Archives.)

John H. Kerlin was born in Fayette County, Georgia, and served in Company I, "Stark Volunteers," 13th Georgia Infantry. John enlisted on May 3, 1862, and surrendered with the unit at Appomattox on April 9, 1865. He is believed to be buried near Tyrone, Georgia. The 13th Georgia was mustered into service on July 8, 1861, at Griffin, Georgia, serving in Floyd's Brigade in West Virginia. It was later reassigned and became part of the famous Lawton-Gordon-Evans Georgia Brigade—Georgia 13th, 26th, 31st, 38th, 60th, and 61st—one of the premiere brigades of the Army of Northern Virginia. (Courtesy of the Fayette County Historical Society.)

Georgians looked to their regimental colors with a sense of pride. From a practical sense, flags were used as gathering points and alignment. This image is taken from a plaque purchased to honor the author's great-great-grandfather, Pvt. Henry B. Dempsey, a member of Company D, "Cherokee Brown Rangers," 14th Georgia Infantry, who died on the surgeon's table during an arm amputation. The few remaining regimental flags are "honored veterans" in private collections, smaller historical centers, Virginia's Museum of the Confederacy, and the Georgia State Capitol Flag Collection. The 14th, 35th, 45th, and 49th made up the Thomas' Brigade, A. P. Hill's Division, "Stonewall" Jackson's Corps, Army of Northern Virginia.

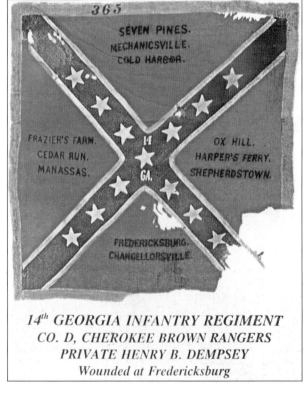

14ᵗʰ GEORGIA INFANTRY REGIMENT
CO. D, CHEROKEE BROWN RANGERS
PRIVATE HENRY B. DEMPSEY
Wounded at Fredericksburg

This image depicts a Culver brother—either Henry or Thomas. Both served as officers of the 15th Georgia Infantry. Henry was wounded and disabled at Second Manassas, while Thomas was killed at the Wilderness on May 6, 1864. Lieutenant Culver wears a nine-button frock coat with a sash around his waist. He holds an eagle-headed sword and wears a slouch hat with five-pointed star and tassel. The 15th later served with distinction at the Battle of Gettysburg and surrendered at Appomattox with the Army of Northern Virginia. (Courtesy of David W. Vaughan.)

Both Tennent brothers from Elbert County, Georgia, enlisted as privates on July 15, 1861, in Company I, "McIntosh Volunteers," of the 15th Georgia Infantry. Henry A. Tennent (left) was captured at Gettysburg but was later exchanged. Orville T. Tennent was appointed corporal in 1863 and later sergeant. The 15th served at Malvern Hill, Second Manassas, Sharpsburg, Gettysburg, Fredericksburg, Chickamauga, Wilderness, Cold Harbor, Petersburg, and Appomattox, where it surrendered. During the war, it served under two Georgia generals, Robert Toombs and Henry Benning. Although in the same unit, the brothers wear different colored uniforms. (Courtesy of Sam Pyle and McDaniel-Curtis SCV Camp.)

One of Georgia's most prominent citizens and political leaders, Maj. Gen. Howell Cobb is shown in a rare image in his Confederate uniform. Entering the army as a colonel of the 16th Georgia Infantry, he was promoted to brigadier general in February 1862 and major general in September 1863. He finished the war in Georgia, organizing the Georgia State Guard and Georgia Reserve Force. He died while on a business trip in New York City in 1868 and is buried in Oconee Hill Cemetery in Athens, Georgia. See page 2 for more information. (Courtesy of David W. Vaughan.)

Augustus C. Thompson, born in Georgia in 1828, was elected captain of Company G, "Jackson County Volunteers," 16th Georgia Infantry, "Sallie Twiggs Regiment," on July 20, 1861. Wounded at the Battle at Crampton's Gap, Maryland, on September 14, 1862, he resigned on August 1, 1863. Three other Thompsons served in the company: A. M. was killed at Crampton's Gap; Milton was captured at Cedar Creek, Virginia, in October 1864 and released at the end of the war; and W. S. was injured in 1864. Other major engagements of the 16th included Malvern Hill, Fredericksburg, Chancellorsville, Gettysburg, and Fort Loudon. (Courtesy of Jackson County Historical Society.)

Passed down through the Bray family, this 1/6 plate ambrotype shows Cpl. Ezekial Bray. He joined Company A, "Madison County Greys," 16th Georgia Infantry. In the Battle of Seven Pines, Virginia, he was hit in the thigh by grapeshot. Even though his wound healed, he was unable to return to active service and served as a nurse until the war's end. Because he never regained full use of his leg, the injury plagued him the rest of his life. Here, he wears a homespun jacket with two handmade bone buttons and one brass button. (Courtesy of David W. Vaughan.)

Dilmus Lyle Jarrett was elected captain of Company C, "Jackson County Volunteers," 18th Georgia Infantry, on April 30, 1861. Mortally wounded at Second Manassas in Virginia on August 30, 1862, he died on September 6, 1862. Under the direction of Colonel Wofford, later a brigadier general, the 18th lost 19 men and had 114 wounded in the engagement. They captured the flags of the 24th and the 10th New York. At Sharpsburg, the 18th lost 57 percent of the unit. Other major engagements included Fredericksburg, Chancellorsville, Gettysburg, Chickamauga, and Fort Loudon. (Courtesy of Jackson County Historical Society.)

33

William Riley Brock, the son of Isaac Brock (who fathered 17 children), was born on February 15, 1839, in Paulding County, Georgia. Living in Van Wert, Georgia, he enlisted as a private on February 23, 1862, in Company K, "Rowland's Infantry," 18th Georgia Infantry, in Bartow County. Having served for the duration of the war, he and his wife, Sarah Huffman Brock, had eight children. In 1904, he and other survivors in Polk County received their Cross of Honor at the Opera House in Cedartown. He died on November 10, 1921, and is buried at Friendship Baptist Church, Cedartown. He is the author's great-great-grandfather.

The Johnson-Jones family gathered in June 1862 near Richmond, Virginia. From left to right are (seated) Dabney Jones; Grandpa J. H. Johnson; unidentified; assistant surgeon Gabe Jones; possibly Maj. Andrew J. Hutchens; Mrs. Thomas Johnson holding the hand of her husband, Lt. Col. Thomas Johnson; the Johnson children in front; and Johnson's brother Lt. William Johnson; (standing) ? Peek, four unidentified, Sgt. R. A. Johnson, and a young servant peering over Sergeant Johnson's shoulders. They were in Georgia's 19th Infantry, many from Company C, "Palmetto Guards." Lieutenant Colonel Johnson was later killed at Mechanicsville, and his brother William at Olustee, Florida. (Courtesy of Robert W. Woodruff Library, Emory University.)

Brothers Moses and Isham Morris enlisted on June 22, 1861, in Carroll County as privates with Company I, "Villa Rica Gold Diggers," 19th Georgia Infantry. The 1860 census shows Moses was 18, living with his parents and siblings. His brother died in Virginia in 1861, but Moses survived the war and surrendered in North Carolina in 1865. Moses poses in his matching light-colored uniform. His belt features a cap box, a frame belt buckle, a bayonet in a scabbard, and a cartridge box. He stands with his rifle and bayonet. (Courtesy of Fred Spake and McDaniel-Curtis SCV Camp.)

Mark Swain was born on December 23, 1838, and was a farmer in Telfair County, Georgia. He enlisted as a third corporal on June 6, 1861, in Company H, "Telfair Volunteers," 20th Georgia Infantry. The 20th was assigned duty as part of the Army of Northern Virginia in August 1861, and it served in Early's, Toombs's, and Benning's Brigades. Its major actions included the Seven Days' Battles; Second Manassas; Gettysburg, where the battle flag took 87 holes; and Chickamauga, where 17 of the 23 officers were wounded or killed. Corporal Swain survived the war and died on October 21, 1881. (Courtesy of Dewey S. Jones, great-grandson of Mark.)

John Thomas Boykin Jr. became captain of Company F, "Ben Hill Volunteers" from Troup County, 21st Georgia Infantry, on July 9, 1861. He resigned because of disability on May 31, 1862. The 21st was one of the first regiments formed in 1861. It has the distinction of having the most wounded or killed in a single battle by a Georgia regiment, losing 76 percent of the 242 engaged at Second Manassas. The unit also took major casualties at Sharpsburg and Chancellorsville and was cited for distinction at Gettysburg. Captain Boykin died on June 25, 1901, in Troup County at the age of 52. (Courtesy of Troup County Archives.)

The six Jones brothers served in the 22nd Georgia Infantry as field officers and members of Company G, the "Fireside Defenders" from Bartow and Floyd Counties. From left to right are (seated) surgeon James (or John) William Jones, Col. Robert H. Jones, Capt. John Joseph Jones; (standing) chaplain W. E. Jones, Lt. Wesley F. Jones, and Cpl. Parks Jones. Col. R. H. Jones and Lt. W. F. Jones were wounded at Sharpsburg in 1862; Lt. W. F. Jones died from his wounds. Capt. J. J. Jones was the father of the world-famous evangelist Sam P. Jones. (Courtesy of Sam Pyle and McDaniel-Curtis SCV Camp.)

Pvt. Noah Jordan volunteered on October 21, 1861, as a member of Company G, "Cherokee Field Guards," 23rd Georgia Infantry. The 23rd were veterans of the Peninsular and Maryland campaigns, but many were captured at the Battle of Chancellorsville. Jordan served with the regiment until he was discharged at James Island, South Carolina, on November 10, 1863. He poses in a dark kepi or "bummers cap" and an eight-button shell jacket with matching trousers. (Courtesy of David W. Vaughan.)

Believed to be brothers, James H. (left) and George W. Douglas(s) joined as privates in Company A, "Thomasville Guards," 29th Georgia Infantry, on July 26, 1861. James was detailed as a machinist to the Macon Arsenal on June 21, 1862. He died of consumption at Macon on February 26, 1864. George was admitted to the Floyd House and Ocmulgee Hospitals at Macon on September 29, 1863. No further information is known about him. The 29th served in the Chickamauga and Atlanta campaigns. On April 9, 1865, the 29th was consolidated into the First Confederate Battalion, and it surrendered at Greensboro, North Carolina. (Courtesy of Thomas County Historical Society, Thomasville, Georgia.)

The Thomasville Zouaves were created in the summer of 1860, taking the look made famous by the French units of the same name. The image in color shows a green jacket with red pants. In February 1861, the company adopted a simple uniform and became the "Ochlockonee Light Infantry." On the right is Thomas Spalding Paine, who had attended Georgia Military Institute in Marietta. He was first lieutenant of Company B, "O.L.I," 29th Georgia Infantry, until his resignation on May 7, 1862. On July 20, 1863, he was elected captain of Company E, 20th Battalion Georgia Cavalry. (Courtesy of Thomas County Historical Society, Thomasville, Georgia.)

Born in Fayette County, Georgia, on September 8, 1845, Sherman Glass Dickson enlisted in Jonesboro on September 25, 1861, at age 16. He enlisted in Company E, "Clayton Invincibles," 30th Georgia Infantry. Wounded at the Battle of Chickamauga on September 19, 1863, he was accidentally killed at the Peebles home in Henry County, Georgia, on February 25, 1865. He is buried in the Glass-Dickson Cemetery in Rivers Edge Development, Clayton County, Georgia. Private Dickson wears a dark slouch hat and displays a large Bowie knife. (Courtesy of John W. Lynch, great-great-nephew of Dickson.)

Frances C. Ray is listed in the 1860 census as 18 years old, born in Georgia, and living with his parents and siblings in Carroll County, Georgia. He enlisted as a private on September 25, 1861, in Company K, "Chattahoochee Volunteers," 30th Georgia Infantry. Two years and one day later, he died of typhoid fever at his home in Carroll County and is buried in the Brown Cemetery. He poses for the photograph wearing sergeant stripes. (Courtesy of Carter Clay and McDaniel-Curtis SCV Camp.)

James C. Doster, son of Wilson and Ellender Waggoner Doster, enlisted as a private on September 5, 1862, in Company A, "Jasper Blues," 32nd Georgia Infantry, at Battery Harrison, Savannah. He was killed at the Battle of Olustee on February 20, 1864. The pension records of his wife, Talitha Kent Doster, indicate he was "shot and killed dead." His remains were sent home. While he was lying in state, one of his five children, 14-month-old son William, took his first steps ever—towards the coffin. William had been named for James's brother, William P. Doster, who had died on September 2, 1862, at Battery Harrison. (Courtesy of Jackson E. Malcom Jr.)

Born in Newton County, Georgia, on May 4, 1837, Pvt. Jordan T. Smith enlisted on May 13, 1862, in Company C, 34th Georgia Infantry. This company was made of men from Coweta and Troup Counties. Smith was captured and paroled while serving at Vicksburg, Mississippi, in July 1864. During the war, his feet were frostbitten so badly that he was disabled for life. In his old age, he would sit in his rocking chair and often be heard repeating, "Damn Yankees, Damn Yankees!" He died on November 24, 1927, and is buried in Union Camp Ground Cemetery in Carroll County. (Courtesy of Fred Spake and McDaniel-Curtis SCV Camp.)

Brothers Pvt. Thomas L. (left) and Charles N. Baker enlisted in Heard County on September 23, 1861, in Company D, 35th Georgia Infantry. Thomas was killed and Charles severely wounded at the Battle of Seven Pines, Virginia, on May 31, 1862. Charles stayed with the unit and was appointed fourth sergeant in December 1862, second sergeant in 1863, and back to private in 1864. Here, Charles holds a D-Guard Bowie knife. During the last days of the war, he was the enrolling captain of Beal's Battalion Georgia State Troops. (Courtesy of Jack Shirey, Sam Pyle, and McDaniel-Curtis SCV Camp.)

Pvt. William Purcell enlisted on May 10, 1862, in Company C, "Franklin Rangers," 9th Battalion Georgia Infantry. The 9th and 3rd Battalions joined to form the 37th Georgia in 1863. Captured and paroled at Hartwell, Georgia, on May 19, 1864, he was wounded in the thigh by a piece of shell at Decatur, Alabama, on November 24, 1864, becoming permanently disabled. After a three-month hospital stay, he was discharged and sent home. He died on February 14, 1911. He wears here a simple frock coat with an unusually high collar. (Courtesy of David W. Vaughan.)

Lt. Thomas H. Bomar, son of Atlanta's second mayor, Dr. Benjamin Bomar, was born in Macon in 1842. The image of Lieutenant Bomar shows him wearing his full dress cadet uniform of the Georgia Military Institute, Marietta. His shako features the Georgia state seal and eagle and ostrich plumes. He entered Confederate service on April 30, 1861, and commanded Company L, "Wright's Legion," 38th Georgia Infantry. He was promoted to major on July 2, 1863. He was captured at Cedar Creek, Virginia, on October 19, 1864, and imprisoned until his release on July 24, 1865. (Courtesy of David W. Vaughan.)

William Ezra Curtis, son of Henry and Nancy Curtis, was born in Georgia in 1827. Elected captain of Company F, 19th Georgia Infantry from Carroll County, he became lieutenant colonel of the 41st Regiment on March 20, 1862, at the death of another Carroll Countian, Col. Charles McDaniel. Promoted to colonel on October 31, 1862, Curtis was captured at Vicksburg and later paroled. Mortally wounded at Mill Creek Gap, Georgia, on February 25, 1864, he was taken to his in-laws' home in Coweta County. His dying wish was to be buried facing the enemy, and he is buried in the Carrollton City Cemetery facing north. The McDaniel-Curtis SCV Camp is named in their honor. (Courtesy of Sam Pyle and McDaniel-Curtis SCV Camp.)

Noah Richard Brogdon was born in Gwinnett County, Georgia, on June 22, 1830. The son of George and Sarah Jackson, he married Harriett Stickland of Forsyth and had one daughter and four sons. On January 2, 1862, Noah accepted a commission as second lieutenant, Company A, "Gwinnett Beauregards," 42nd Georgia Infantry. After training at Big Shanty, Georgia, his regiment traveled to Cumberland Gap, Tennessee, where he contracted mumps and died on June 27, 1862. Harriett and his brother Hope retrieved his body by wagon. He is buried at Level Creek Methodist Church in Suwanee. (Courtesy of Lisa K. Kennedy, great-great-great-granddaughter of Noah.)

Elijah Henry Clarke enlisted as a private on March 4, 1862, in Company D, "DeKalb Rangers," 42nd Georgia Infantry. He rose in ranks, being elected second lieutenant in 1862, first lieutenant in 1862, and company captain on May 1, 1863. The 42nd was involved in the Vicksburg and Atlanta campaigns. He surrendered with the unit and the Army of Tennessee at Greensboro, North Carolina, on April 26, 1865. He wears an Italian-style fatigue hat and a uniform with black facings and a large stripe on the pants, and he is armed with two different style revolvers. (Courtesy of Photographic Collection, DeKalb History Center.)

Seven Fincher brothers served in the "Zillicofer Guards" of Forsyth County, Company I, 43rd Georgia Infantry. The officer on the right is believed to be Jr. Lt. Jesse C. Fincher with one of his brothers. The other Finchers who served in the unit were Pvt. Joseph L., Pvt. Joseph E., Pvt. E. W., Sgt. John W., Sgt. Elias, and 1st Lt. James C. The 43rd served in operations in Alabama, Vicksburg, Chattanooga-Ringold, Atlanta, North Alabama, and Middle Tennessee, and in the Carolinas campaign. The unit surrendered at Greensboro, North Carolina, on April 26, 1865. (Courtesy of David W. Vaughan.)

Born in Scotland, Peter Alexander Selkirk McGlashan came to the United States in 1848. He joined the Ochlocknee Light Infantry as a private and then sergeant. He then formed Company E, "Thomas County Rangers," 50th Georgia Infantry, part of the Army of Northern Virginia. He was elected captain on October 1, 1862, and colonel on July 31, 1863. He was promoted to brigadier general in March 1865 and captured at Sayler's Creek, Virginia, on April 6, 1865. After the war, he was elected mayor of Thomasville but later moved to Savannah, where he drowned in 1908 and is buried at Laurel Grove Cemetery. (Courtesy of Thomas County Historical Society, Thomasville, Georgia.)

Pvt. Drewry Farrer was born in Henry County, Georgia, on September 7, 1838. He enlisted in Fayetteville, Georgia, on May 1, 1862, in Company C, "Fayette Planters," 53rd Georgia Infantry. He was captured at Farmville, Virginia, on April 6, 1865, shortly before the surrender of the Army of Northern Virginia, and was sent to Point Lookout Prison in Maryland. After his release on June 25, 1865, he returned to Fayette County, married Pamela Banks, and had eight children. He died in Fayette County on February 12, 1898. (Courtesy of John W. Lynch.)

William Baker, son of Matthew and Martha Baker, was born on January 15, 1835. He enlisted as a private in Fayette County on May 1, 1862, in Company C, "Fayette Planters," 53rd Georgia Infantry. At the Battle of Cedar Creek, Virginia, on October 19, 1864, he was shot through the right side, and the ball passed through his thorax. Captured, he remained a prisoner throughout the war. Pictured after returning home, he wears a uniform made by his family. He married Keron Rebecca Pyle and raised six children. He died on August 30, 1894, and is buried with his wife at Harmony Grove Christian Church in Fulton, County. (Courtesy of Sam Pyle and *William Baker Family History* by Virgil D. Baker Jr.)

Moses Ansley was elected captain of Company I, 4th Regiment State Troops on October 25, 1861. Mustered out in April of 1862, he was elected first lieutenant of Company D, 53rd Infantry, on May 6, 1862. The men of Company D were from Coweta and Heard Counties. He became captain on October 27, 1862, and was captured at Knoxville, Tennessee, on November 29, 1863. He was released at Fort Delaware, Delaware, on June 12, 1865. He suffered the rest of his life with bronchitis he contracted in service and died on September 16, 1886. (Courtesy of Male Academy Museum of Newnan-Coweta.)

In 1860, John Turner Barrow, age 28, was listed as living in Carroll County with his wife and child. He enlisted in Carroll County on May 5, 1862, and was appointed third sergeant of Company B, 56th Georgia. The 56th served in the Army of Tennessee and saw action at the recapture of Cumberland Gap and the advance into Kentucky before being sent to defend Vicksburg. Sergeant Barrow died of smallpox in a hospital in Atlanta on February 13, 1863. The 56th later fought at Missionary Ridge, Atlanta, and Tennessee, and finished its service in the Carolinas. (Courtesy of Hugh Barrow and McDaniel-Curtis SCV Camp.)

Cinncinatus "Cince" Saxon Guyton was born on December 2, 1834, in Laurens County. He was elected captain of Company C, 2nd Regiment, 1st Brigade, Georgia State Troops, and then major of the regiment on February 12, 1862. In the spring of 1862, the brigade was reorganized as the 57th Georgia Infantry. On May 24, 1862, Guyton was elected lieutenant colonel of the regiment. Captured at the Battle of Vicksburg, the unit was paroled and later took part in the battles around Kennesaw and Atlanta. The 57th was then assigned duties in Tennessee. Guyton died of a stroke on August 14, 1884. (Courtesy of Laurens County Historical Society.)

Officers of Company H, "Independent Volunteers," 57th Georgia, of Baldwin County relax with their pipes. At left, 1st Lt. Archibald C. McKinley (shoulder) and (second from left) Capt. John R. Bonner (leg) were wounded at Baker's Creek. Captain Bonner was later wounded again at Vining Station on July 4, 1864. William Spivey Stetson (far right) enlisted as a private but rose to the rank of second lieutenant and was severely wounded in the leg at Kennesaw. All three were captured while defending Vicksburg. The servant pouring from the canteen was named Scott. (Courtesy of Special Collections, GC&SU Library, Georgia College & State University.)

Daniel Worsham (or Wisham) was born in Taylor County, Georgia, in 1832. He enlisted on April 9, 1865, with Company C, "Arthur Greys," 59th Georgia Infantry. Daniel surrendered with the 59th and Army of Northern Virginia at Appomattox on April 9, 1865. He died in March 1891 or 1892. Daniel is armed with a long D-Guard Bowie knife. (Courtesy of Museum of Colquitt County History, Jack Bridwell, executive director.)

George Washington Wood, appointed junior second lieutenant, enlisted at Dalton on September 19, 1861, in Company B, "Fannin Guards," 60th Georgia Infantry. For the first part of the war, the 60th was assigned to Lawton's Brigade and later Gordon's Brigade of the Army of Northern Virginia. Lieutenant Wood was wounded at Sharpsburg (Antietam), Maryland, on September 17, 1862; at Gettysburg, he was severely wounded in the liver and lungs. Captured on July 3, 1863, he died of his wounds 20 days later. He wears a double-breasted gray coat with darker collar and cuffs. (Courtesy of David W. Vaughan.)

George Fennell Newton was born in Lowndes, now Brook County, Georgia, on September 21, 1841. He enlisted as a private in Company C, "Wiregrass Rifles," 61st Georgia Infantry on September 7, 1861, in Quitman. He was wounded at Sharpsburg, Maryland, on September 17, 1862. He was also wounded at Gettysburg and required amputation of his arm at the shoulder. He later served in the Georgia legislature. He died on February 6, 1922, and is buried at Pleasant Grove Cemetery in Colquitt County. (Courtesy of Museum of Colquitt County History, Jack Bridwell, executive director.)

The Georgia 66th Infantry Regiment was organized at Atlanta, Georgia, during the summer of 1863. Pvt. George W. Musick enlisted in Company H, 66th Georgia, on November 13, 1863. He was killed at the Battle of Peachtree Creek, Georgia, on July 20, 1864. Sgt. Hamilton Hogan, from his unit, recounted in pension statements seeing Musick's dead body on the battlefield. The homespun uniform with large buttons was characteristic of uniforms in the latter years of the war as a result of shortages. (Courtesy of Fred Spake and McDaniel-Curtis SCV Camp.)

Born in Gwinnett County, Moses Brown was appointed first sergeant of Company E, 7th Georgia Infantry, on May 29, 1861. After being wounded in the left foot at First Manassas on July 21, 1861, he was discharged. On March 22, 1862, he was elected captain of Company E, 66th Georgia Infantry, and on August 1, 1863, he was detailed as a drillmaster at Camp of Instruction, Decatur. Due to his war injury, he was recommended for retirement from field duty and was assigned post duty in one of the staff departments. He died in Decatur on September 26, 1910. (Courtesy of David W. Vaughan.)

Thomas Reade Rootes Cobb was born in Jefferson County, Georgia, on April 10, 1823. He was the brother of Confederate general Howell Cobb and cousin to Gen. Henry Rootes Jackson. After graduating from the University of Georgia, he became a renowned lawyer. He was a delegate at the Confederate Convention in Montgomery, where his brother served as president and he helped write the Confederate Constitution. He was commissioned as a colonel on August 28, 1861, and raised Cobb's Legion. Promoted to brigadier general on November 1, 1862, he was wounded at the Battle of Fredericksburg and died on December 13, 1862. (*Confederate Veteran*, 1899.)

James Henry Lamar Benford, who was born on April 4, 1837, enlisted on July 30, 1861, as a private in Company B, "Bowden Volunteers," Cobb's Legion Infantry, in Bowdon, Georgia. He was discharged disabled on November 21, 1861, but enlisted as a private in June 1862 in Company B, 7th Georgia Cavalry. He then transferred to Company B, 10th Georgia Cavalry. He was paroled on May 10, 1865, in Dalton. He died on September 4, 1904, and is buried at Pleasant Grove Baptist Church Cemetery in Carroll County. (Courtesy of Carter Clay and McDaniel-Curtis SCV Camp.)

Charles Virgil V. Brown was born on July 4, 1842, in Cass County, Georgia. On June 11, 1861, he enlisted as a private in Company D, "Polk County Rifles," Phillip's Legion. Private Brown was wounded at Gettysburg in 1863 and again in 1864. He was furloughed home. Although recovering from wounds, he left to fight in May and was captured while wearing his uniform. Accused of spying by the Federal soldiers, he returned home under guard, was allowed to say goodbye, was removed to an enemy camp at Burnt Hickory, and was executed. The next day his family was allowed to claim the body. (Courtesy of Joanne Kingsbery Craig, great-great-niece of Charles.)

Light Heckleman Wilmoth was 19 when he enlisted in Company M, "Denmead Volunteers," Phillips Legion Infantry, on April 28, 1862, at Marietta. His older brothers Harrison and William J. were members in Company L, "Blackwell Volunteers," Phillips Legion, and had enlisted on April 28, 1862. William was captured at Gettysburg and died of smallpox. Light survived the war but died on April 1, 1886, and is buried in the Marietta City Cemetery. He is shown wearing a nine-button jacket with a book in his right hand. Harrison was captured in Knoxville but survived the war and died in Marietta in 1902. (Courtesy of Marietta Museum of History.)

Capt. Henry Wirz was born in Switzerland in 1823 but moved to Louisiana in 1849. He initially enlisted in the 4th Louisiana Infantry and was wounded at Seven Pines. Promoted to captain, he was sent by Jefferson Davis to deliver dispatches in Europe. In 1864, he became commandant of Andersonville Prison. After the war, he was arrested while under a parole and in time of peace. He was condemned to death by hanging on charges of murder and excessive cruelty. Many today question these charges. This image was taken in Switzerland in 1863 and was donated to the Drummer Boy Museum by Col. Hendrich Wirz, his great-grandnephew. See page 83. (Courtesy of the Drummer Boy Museum and the Andersonville Guild.)

James Longstreet was born in Edgefield District, South Carolina, on January 8, 1821, at his grandmother's home. He was raised until the age of nine on a farm near Gainesville, Georgia. Living with an aunt and uncle in Augusta, he attended Richmond Academy. Longstreet graduated from West Point in 1842 as a second lieutenant. Assigned to the U.S. 4th Infantry at in Missouri, he befriended Ulysses S. Grant there and introduced him to his cousin Julia Dent, whom Grant married. Longstreet served honorably in the Mexican War and received promotions to lieutenant, captain, and major. First appointed a lieutenant colonel in the Confederate Army, he became a brigadier general in 1861. See page 117. (*Century War Book*, 1888.)

John B. Gordon was born on February 6, 1832, in Upson County, Georgia, but moved to Walker County at age eight. He quickly rose through the ranks: captain of company of 6th Alabama (which included Georgians), then major, lieutenant colonel, and colonel. At the Battle of Sharpsburg, he was wounded five times. On November 1, 1862, he was promoted to brigadier general. Gordon's Brigade became the largest in the army and served with distinction at Chancellorsville, Fredericksburg, and Gettysburg. After the Battle of the Wilderness, he was promoted to major general and then led 2nd Corps over half the Army of Northern Virginia. See page 72 and 115. (Courtesy of Library of Congress.)

Born in 1843, Abraham Huddleston "Hud" York was the son of Josiah York, who had served as a constable in Carroll County before moving to Polk County, Georgia. Hud and four brothers enlisted in Company A, 1st Regiment of Georgia Cavalry. The brothers were Capt. William T., who was killed at Peachtree Creek; Sgt. Jasper Newton; Sgt. Larkin B.; and Josiah Jr., who was wounded in the eye at Gettysburg. Hud, his father, and their families donated land on which the Methodist church in Yorkville was built. The community was named for them. Hud and his wife are buried in the Van Wert Methodist Church Cemetery in Van Wert, Georgia. (Courtesy of Glenn T. York Jr., great-grandson of Hud.)

Born April 6, 1832, Pvt. Nathan C. Jones enlisted at Carrollton into Company E, 1st Georgia Cavalry. The 1860 Carroll County census shows him at age 28 living with his wife and two children. He was one of nine sons of Elder Thomas B. and Celia Jones, of which seven served in the Confederate Army. Shot through the upper arm in battle near Dallas, Georgia, in 1864, he was discharged due to the wound and disabled the rest of his life. He is buried in the Jones Cemetery in Carroll County. (Courtesy of Curtis Spivey, Sam Pyle, descendants, and McDaniel-Curtis SCV Camp.)

Samuel H. Deane was born in Griffin, Georgia, on February 22, 1842. He enlisted on February 15, 1862, at Albany, Georgia, in Company E, 2nd Georgia Cavalry. He served under Colonel Lawton and later under Gen. N. B. Forrest. He was in active service for the duration, except for 30 days while imprisoned after being captured at Lebanon Junction, Kentucky. Some of the battles in which he fought include Murfreesboro, Chickamauga, New Hope Church, Resaca, and Kennesaw. He was in the mercantile business and served as a Griffin alderman for 12 years. He died on May 8, 1900, in at his home in Griffin. (*Confederate Veteran*, 1902.)

James Madison Bridges was born on March 15, 1847, in Georgia. At age 16, he joined Confederate service with his father, R. C. Bridges, and younger brother Wiley Jones Bridges. They enlisted in Company E, 2nd Georgia Cavalry, under Gen. Joseph Wheeler. It is said that the boys were part Creek Indian. James was paroled in Greensboro, North Carolina, at the end of the war. He married Antoinette Cobb in 1869, and they had seven children. He died on February 3, 1896, and is buried in the Brooks City Cemetery. (Courtesy of Sue Maglin, great-great-granddaughter of James, and Fayette County Historical Society.)

This image is believed to be Jeffrey (Jefferey) Youngblood Beck, son of Isaiah Beck Jr., born in July 1826. He was a private in Company G, 2nd Georgia Cavalry State Guards. He would have been about 38 years old in 1864 when the cavalry unit was formed. He had two other brothers who served, Seymore Y. in Company B, "Bowden Volunteers," Cobb's Legion, and Isaiah Springer Beck, a third sergeant in Company I, "Heard County Rangers," 41st Georgia Infantry. (Courtesy of Fred Spake and McDaniel-Curtis SCV Camp.)

Lt. Col. James Thomas Thornton is posed in his uniform in 1862. He convinced about 25 of his friends and neighbors to go from Stewart County to Columbus, Georgia, the nearest reporting station. Since they had their own horses, they were placed in the cavalry. Elected captain by the men of Company E, 3rd Georgia Cavalry, in May 1962, he was later promoted to lieutenant colonel. The 3rd served under Generals N. B. Forrest and Joseph Wheeler. The unit participated in more than 200 engagements, with major action at Stones River, Tullahoma, Chickamauga, Chattanooga, and Atlanta. Lt. Col. Jack Thornton signed the surrender papers for General Wheeler at Greensboro, North Carolina. (Courtesy of Jack Thornton, Lt. Col. Tom Nelson Camp SCV.)

Born in Macon in 1826, surgeon Joseph Barnett Carlton graduated from the University of Georgia and became a physician in Athens. At the outbreak of the war, Dr. Carlton first volunteered with the 2nd Battalion Georgia State Troops until the unit disbanded in May 1862. Hearing of the devastation at the Seven Days' Battles in Virginia, he went to Richmond and volunteered his services where needed. Returning to Georgia, he joined Company F, "Toombs Cavalry," 3rd Cavalry Georgia State Guards. He is posed in a double-breasted frock coat, with major insignia; the coat features black cuffs and collar indicating Confederate Medical Department. (Courtesy of David W. Vaughan.)

David Franklin Tisinger, a wheelwright by trade, was a private in Company C and K in the 3rd Georgia Cavalry Regiment. He later transferred to the 20th Georgia Light Artillery. Detailed to work in the quartermaster shop at Columbus, Georgia, he used his pre-war skills in repairing wagon wheels. He is posed in a standard, light-colored, seven-button coat with cavalry saber. (Courtesy of Carter Clay and McDaniel-Curtis SCV Camp.)

Pvt. Thomas H. Tate joined Company B, "Hall Chattahoochee Cavalry," 4th Regiment Georgia State Guards, the "Blue Ridge Tiger Regiment," in 1863. Thomas Tate was born in Athens on May 22, 1844, and was 17 at the time of this image. Although records do not show any service prior to 1863, the image from May 1861 shows him wearing a Confederate uniform. He is dressed in a gray, eight-button, shelled jacket trimmed with dark facing and two side pockets. He holds a flower in his left hand. (Courtesy of David W. Vaughan.)

William Madison "Dock" Trippe was born February 4, 1840, in Cherokee County. He enlisted as a private in Company C, "Cherokee Dragons," 4th Georgia State Brigade's Cavalry Battalion, at Camp McDonald on June 22, 1861. In August, the battalion became part of the Phillips Legion. According to family stories, Dock is posing here at the time of his marriage to Elizabeth Ann Davis in Polk County, while on furlough on August 27, 1863. He surrendered with the legion at Greensboro, North Carolina. He died on January 12, 1926, at Taylorsville and is buried in the Taylorsville Cemetery. (Courtesy of Dr. Robert E. Davis.)

John David Cay was born in Liberty County, Georgia, on September 17, 1840. David enlisted in Captain Walthour's Liberty Independent Troop, 1st Georgia Volunteer Cavalry Battalion, which was formed in 1861. On January 20, 1863, the 1st and 2nd Georgia Cavalry Battalions joined to create the 5th Georgia Cavalry. Private Cay was appointed second corporal. He was captured in late 1864 at his father's home in Walthourville, Liberty County, Georgia. He posed for this image in October 1864 in a coat and hat his mother had made from a blanket. Twigs were used as buttons (Courtesy of State of Florida Archives.)

Robert William DeLoach, along with his brother Z. Taylor DeLoach, was a member of Company E, 5th Georgia Cavalry. The regiment, formed by the consolidation of the 1st and 2nd Georgia Cavalry Battalions on January 20, 1863, served under Gen. Joseph Wheeler's command. After the war, the brothers went into business together, owning DeLoach's Mill. Robert later served in the state legislature and died on March 4, 1930, at age 87. (Courtesy of Smith Callaway Banks, Bulloch County historian and Special Collections, Henderson Library, Georgia Southern University.)

The proclaimed youngest regular Confederate, David Bailey Freeman was born on May 1, 1851, in Ellijay, Gilmer County, Georgia. He was a son of Beverly and Mary Freeman, who had 10 children, 8 of whom were boys. Madison, an older brother, raised a cavalry company in Gilmer County, and David accompanied him as an aide. In his own words, he said, "I went in at ten, entering in April, 1862, as marker for the 6th Georgia Cavalry; but as there was practically no drilling to do, in a month or two I was in the regular ranks, and did all the duties of a soldier . . . unless legitimately on some detachment or other mission, never missed an engagement . . . which was nearly three years. . . . I was armed with a short saber and two saddle pistols." See page 114.

59

Stephen Pollard (1830–1899) was born in Fayette County, Georgia, and was the oldest son of Irvin Pollard. Prior to the war, he moved to Carroll County, where he met and married Mary Ann Vines. They then moved to Haralson County. Stephen served as a private in the 7th Confederate Cavalry, Partisan Rangers, and later served in the 40th Georgia Infantry. He surrendered at Greensboro on April 26, 1865. He poses in a light-colored overshirt with a dark collar, cuffs, and shoulder lapels. He is armed with an 1855 U.S. single-shot pistol with shoulder stock and a pair of revolvers. He is buried at Liberty Christian Church in Temple, Georgia. (Courtesy of Fayette County Historical Society.)

Charles A. Hires was born in 1825 and served with Company I, 62nd Cavalry Regiment Partisan Rangers. This regiment was also known as the 2nd Partisan Rangers Regiment. It was formed from seven Georgia and three North Carolina companies. Men from Georgia were from Dougherty, Liberty, and Baker Counties. The Adjutant and Inspector General's Office split the regiment on July 11, 1864, with the Georgia companies going to the 8th Cavalry Regiment. Private Hires is buried at Sardis Church in Colquitt County. (Courtesy of Museum of Colquitt County History, Jack Bridwell, executive director.)

Henry Francis Jones, son of Tom and Lavinia Jones of Greenwood Plantation, lived in Thomas County, Georgia. A graduate of the University of North Carolina, he entered law school at the University of Georgia. Upon secession, he and classmates joined Cobb's Legion. Organized in the spring of 1861 and composed of cavalry, infantry, and artillery, the legion moved to Virginia. In the cavalry, Henry reached the rank of first lieutenant but died on July 12, 1864, from injuries sustained when an artillery shell hit him and two other soldiers. His body was returned home. (Courtesy of Thomas County Historical Society, Thomasville, Georgia.)

William Gaston Delony was a lawyer from Athens when the war started. Entering service as a captain in Cobb's Legion, he became a lieutenant colonel in 1862. He was involved in the largest cavalry battle of the war at Brandy Station and was wounded at Gettysburg on July 3, 1863, receiving several saber blows to the face, from which it took two months to recuperate. Fighting at Jack's Shop in Virginia, he was wounded by a mini ball in the thigh on September 22. Captured, he died at age 34 in a Washington, D.C., hospital after the wound turned gangrenous. (Courtesy of David W. Vaughan.)

Pvt. William Clayton Hood, born in Jackson County in 1837, was a member of Company H, Cobb's Legion Cavalry. This cavalry served with the Army of Northern Virginia. Although official records indicate that this cavalry was to be designated in July 1864 as the 9th Regiment Georgia Cavalry, the order was apparently never carried out. Living in Jackson County into his 80s, he died in 1922. Private Hood poses in a light-colored shell jacket with matching pants that have a small stripe. He wears a dark bow tie and is armed with a cavalry saber and revolver. (Courtesy of Jackson County Historical Society.)

Pierce Manning Butler Young moved to Cass County, Georgia, in 1838 at the age of two. He attended the Georgia Military Institute in 1852. Appointed to West Point in 1857, he remained a cadet until Georgia seceded. Appointed a second lieutenant of artillery, he quickly rose through the ranks. On September 5, 1862, he became a lieutenant colonel in Cobb's Legion Cavalry. While leading a charge at the Battle of Brandy Station on June 9, 1863, he was wounded in the chest. On September 28, 1863, he was promoted to brigadier general in J. E. B. Stuart's Cavalry Corps. Note the uniform of a brigadier. (Courtesy of David W. Vaughan.)

General Young was again wounded in the chest at the Battle of Hanover Courthouse, Virginia, on May 30, 1864. In November, he was reassigned to defend Georgia and oppose Sherman. He was promoted to major general on December 30, 1864, and commanded a cavalry division in Georgia and the Carolinas until the war's end. He later served as a U.S. congressman from 1868 to 1875 and held several government positions including consul general to Russia. He died on July 6, 1896, and is buried in Oak Hill Cemetery in Cartersville. Note the difference between this and the previous image. He poses in the triple-button arrangement of a major general. (Courtesy of David W. Vaughan.)

Joseph Wheeler, "Fighting Joe," was born in 1836 in Augusta, Georgia. Graduating from West Point in 1859, he rose through the ranks: first lieutenant of artillery, 19th Alabama Infantry colonel, commander of the brigade, cavalry commander, brigadier general in October 1862, major general in January 1863, and lieutenant general in February 1865. He distinguished himself at Shiloh, Murfreesboro, Perryville, Chickamauga, and Atlanta. He was wounded three times and lost 16 horses. After the war, he served as a U.S. congressman from Alabama and as a major general in the U.S. Army during the Spanish-American War. He died in 1906 and is buried at Arlington National Cemetery in Washington, D.C. (Courtesy of Library of Congress.)

This image is of an unidentified private of the "Washington Artillery," 1st Independent Georgia Battalion, Army of Tennessee. He wears a gray, seven-button frock coat with tinted red cuffs and collar. His dark kepi has "WA" for the Washington Artillery, and the first national flag is pinned on top of his kepi. The W. A., an independent company, was reassigned several times: Company F, 36th Infantry, Burtwell's Battery, and then Pritchard's Battery. It participated in Shiloh, Murfreesboro, Jonesboro, and Nashville, and the Corinth, Kentucky, and Atlanta campaigns, finishing the war in North Carolina. (Courtesy of David W. Vaughan.)

Edwin Harrison Guess became a second lieutenant in Company B, Fulton Artillery, 9th Georgia Light Artillery Battalion. The battalion first served in Georgia before transferring to Tennessee. It was in action in southwest Virginia and in the Knoxville, Tennessee, campaign. The battalion then transferred to the Department of Richmond in 1864 and was stationed at Chaffin's Bluff, Virginia. The battalion participated in the Petersburg siege and served as infantry under Gen. Clement Evans in the Appomattox campaign. It surrendered with the Army of Northern Virginia. (Courtesy of Photographic Collection, DeKalb History Center.)

Pvt. George M. Harper enlisted in Americus on September 10, 1861, in Company A, "Cutts Battery," 11th Battalion Georgia Artillery, the "Sumter Flying Artillery." As part of the Army of Northern Virginia, he was present and counted for in all battles and engagements. At the end of May near Totopotomoy Creek, Virginia, he was wounded and recuperated at Hospital No. 9 in Richmond. He wears a loose gray-blue uniform with sergeant stripes and crooked crossed cannons on the kepi, implying that he may have borrowed the uniform for the picture. (Courtesy of David W. Vaughan.)

William Henry K. Martin, the young soldier on the right, was born on June 20, 1848. He enlisted in the 11th Battalion Georgia Light Artillery, "Sumter Battalion," on March 13, 1862, as a private at the age of 13 years, 8 months. The 11th fought with the Army of Northern Virginia. After the war, William was active in the Irvin Guard Survivor's Association. He died on December 7, 1935, and is buried in Washington, Georgia. Believed to be Henry's uncle, Cpl. George Kitto (left), was in the same unit and was killed in service. (Courtesy of Randy Fleming, great-great-grandson of William.)

Andrew P. Brown was a second lieutenant in Company A, "Newnan Guards," Ramsey's 1st Georgia Infantry. This company was received into service on June 10, 1861, near Richmond, Virginia. Lieutenant Brown mustered out at Augusta, Georgia, on March 18, 1862; he was elected second lieutenant of 2nd Company A, 12th Battalion, Georgia Light Artillery, on May 1, 1862, and first lieutenant on November 6, 1862. He was killed at Fort Sumter, South Carolina, on October 28, 1863. He wears a Confederate artillery officer's uniform in the photograph with red collar, cuffs, and sash. (Courtesy of Male Academy Museum of Newnan-Coweta.)

James Daniel Brock enlisted as a private on May 1, 1862, in Company A, "Newnan Artillery" from Coweta County, 12th Georgia Battalion Light Artillery. He was killed in the Battle of Cold Harbor, Virginia, on June 2, 1864, leaving a widow and several children. Years later, Y. H. Thompson, S. S. Conyers, and J. E. Robinson stated that they were present when he was shot through the head and they helped bury him on the battlefield. A memorial headstone was placed by his wife's grave at Pleasant View Baptist Church by the McDaniel-Curtis Camp of Carrollton. (Courtesy of Sam Pyle and McDaniel-Curtis SCV Camp.)

This image of the King brothers from Houston County was taken in April 1862. From left to right are (seated) Francis Marion King and Alfred Augustus King; (standing) John Hamblin (Hamlin) King, and Sylvester Capers King. Corporals Francis and Alfred and Sergeant Sylvester served as members of the "Southern Rights Guards," Company C., Ramsey's 1st Georgia Infantry, until it disbanded in March 1862. Francis was later a private in Company B, 2nd Regiment South Carolina Artillery; Alfred and Sylvester joined Company A, 14th Battalion Georgia Light Artillery; and John served with Company G, "Silver Greys," State Troops. Wesley, another brother, died in service. (Courtesy of Susan Patton Hamersky, great-great-grandniece.)

Edward Porter Alexander was born in Washington, Georgia, on May 26, 1835. He graduated from West Point with the class of 1857. Resigning from the U.S. Army on May 1, 1861, he accepted an appointment as a Confederate captain of engineers. He became the chief of ordnance of the Army of Northern Virginia and chief artillerist for Longstreet's Corps and was appointed brigadier general on February 26, 1864, one of three artillerists to do so. Severely wounded at Petersburg, he died in Savannah on April 28, 1910, and is buried at Augusta's Magnolia Cemetery. He was the brother-in-law to Generals Jeremy Gilmer and Alexander Lawton, two fellow Georgians. (*Confederate Military History, Georgia,* 1899.)

Josiah Tattnal III was born on November 9, 1795, on the family estate, Bonaventure, in Savannah. The son of a Revolutionary War hero and Georgia governor, he served in the U.S. Navy during the War of 1812, Algerian War, Mexican War, and Opium War, rising to the rank of commodore. After secession, he became the senior flag officer of the Georgia Navy and then captain in the Confederate States Navy (CSN). He commanded the Mosquito Fleet on Georgia's coast, then the CSS *Virginia* (*Merrimac*) in Virginia, and then back to Georgia's defense where he was captured. He died in Savannah on June 14, 1871, and is buried at Bonaventure Cemetery, part of his family's estate. Capt. John R. F. Tattnal of the Confederate States Marine Corps is also buried here in the family plot. (Courtesy of U.S. Naval Historical Center.)

John McIntosh Kell was born in 1823 in McIntosh County, Georgia. He entered the U.S. Navy in 1841 as a midshipman and participated in the Mexican War and in Commodore Perry's expedition to Japan. After secession, he commanded the Georgia gunboat *Savannah* but received a commission in the CSN as a first lieutenant. He was assigned to Comdr. Raphael Semmes, became executive officer on the CSS *Sumter,* and then served on the CSS *Alabama* until her sinking. Promoted to commander, he commanded the ironclad CSS *Richmond.* He died in 1900 and is buried in the Griffin City Cemetery. (Courtesy of U.S. Naval Historical Center.)

Two

Some Came Home
and We Remembered

This image and the one to follow are the oldest known images of a Confederate Memorial Day celebration. Although unclear as to which individual is most responsible, it is clear that Miss Lizzie Rutherford (Ellis), Mrs. Charles J. Williams, and the other ladies of Columbus contributed. The image reads, "Presented to the Ladies Memorial Association by L. J. Abbott. The Columbus Guards, First Decoration of Soldiers Graves in Linwood Cemetery, Columbus, Georgia, April 26, 1866." (Courtesy of Chattahoochee Valley Photograph Collection, Columbus State University Archives.)

The Columbus Light Guards honored the marking of the graves with flowers on this first recognized celebration in Columbus and the beginning of Memorial Day in Georgia. Other communities around the state had early observances: a Georgia historical marker in Kingston tells of an observance in late April 1865, a year earlier, and claims to the oldest continuous observance in the nation with credit to the Darden family and others. Atlanta, Macon, Resaca, and Marietta also had early documented observances. (Courtesy of Chattahoochee Valley Photograph Collection, Columbus State University Archives.)

Mrs. Mary Ann Williams was the wife of Col. C. J. Williams, 1st Georgia Regulars. Colonel Williams, former Georgia Speaker of the House, died in Virginia in 1862. His body was brought home, and Mrs. Williams honored his grave with flowers. She died in 1874 and was buried with military honors in Columbus. Her letter dated March 12, 1866, published throughout the South, calls upon the ladies to "keep alive the memory of the debt we owe them, by dedicating at least one day in each year to embellishing their humble graves with flowers." The ladies of the South answered her call. (*History of Georgia*, 1881.)

Gen. Paul J. Semmes was born in Wilkes County, Georgia, on June 14, 1815. Having served as a captain of the Columbus Guards from 1846 until the outbreak of the war, he became a colonel of the 2nd Georgia Infantry and was promoted to brigadier general on March 11, 1862. He was critically wounded at Gettysburg on July 2, 1863, and died July 10. The image shows veterans honoring General Semmes when his body was returned to Columbus for interment. A slab purchased by the Children of the Confederacy was placed on the grave in 1904. (Courtesy of Chattahoochee Valley Photograph Collection, Columbus State University Archives.)

Veterans and ladies in the background stand at attention in this photograph. Believed to have been taken sometime in the 1880s, this image is believed to show veterans at a reunion of the 41st Georgia in Carroll County. The 41st had two companies of Carroll County men. Two commanders from Carroll were killed while serving: Col. Charles McDaniel died from wounds at Perryville, Kentucky, on October 17, 1862, and Col. William Curtis died near Atlanta on July 25, 1864. The McDaniel-Curtis SCV Camp is named for them. Some believe that Maj. William McDaniel, Company B, Cobb's Legion, nephew of Col. Charles McDaniel, is at the forefront. (Courtesy of Jim and Judy Rowell.)

J. L. McCollum, superintendent of the Western & Atlantic Railroad and former member of the "Raccoon Roughs," held a reunion at his home in 1889. The unit had men from the Raccoon Mountains in Northeast Georgia. The company was comprised of men from Georgia, Alabama, and Tennessee, and they wore coonskin caps. They became a part of the Sixth Alabama Infantry. Gen. John B. Gordon, original company captain, can be seen wearing a coonskin on his chest under the banner that features his portrait (see pages 53 and 115). (*Confederate Veteran*, 1898.)

Veterans from Emanuel and Johnson Counties gathered at Kite, Georgia, in 1890. The photograph identifies them from left to right—with one too many names on the back row—as follows: (first row) Jack Williams, Tom Sharp, George W. Schwalls, Will Mayo, unidentified, John Ellis, unidentified, Charles Wheeler, John P. Mixon, Andrew Sheley, Jimmy Anderson, Richard Mixon, and Andrew Atkinson; (second row) Harold Horton, Press Williams, Bennett Powell, Minter Burns, Math Bell, D. Z. Douglas, Arch Woods, Preacher Ben Fortner, H. G. Neal, B. Y. Wheeler, Capt. John D. Martin, unidentified, C. T. J. Claxton, George Inman, John E. Meadows, Henry G. Wheeler, D. T. Johnson, Ramsey Powell, Jim Peebles, Jordan Norris, and Obbie Fortner. (Courtesy of Thad and Brian Beckham.)

A Confederate reunion was held at the Fayette County Courthouse in 1891. Identified in the back row are Edward C. Stephens (third from left), Andrew J. McBride (seventh from right), and John W. Kitchens (first on right); Ross M. Henderson is in the center of the second row. On the back of the photo is written, "Presented by John W. Kitchens to R. H. (N.) Bennett, September 21, 1891." (Courtesy of John W. Lynch.)

Veterans from Bartow and Floyd Counties that made up Company G, "Fireside Volunteers," 22nd Georgia Infantry, met at Lindale, Georgia, on August 14, 1895. The 22nd saw action at Seven Days' Battles, the campaign in Northern Virginia, Sharpsburg, Fredericksburg, Chancellorsville, Gettysburg, and Southeastern Virginia and North Carolina. Many of the company were wounded and killed at King's School House, Virginia, on June 25, 1862, and at the Crater near Petersburg on July 30, 1864. (Courtesy of Rome Area History Museum.)

The platform of the second annual meeting of the Georgia Daughters of the Confederacy is shown in Augusta, Georgia, in 1897. Seated from left to right are Rev. Lansing Burrows; Miss Rosa Woodberry of Athens; Mrs. R. E. Park, vice-president, from Macon; Mrs. W. F. Eve, president, from Augusta; Mrs. Randolph Ridgeley, secretary; and Mrs. L. H. Rogers, secretary. Overhead are portraits of Jefferson Davis, Stonewall Jackson, and Robert E. Lee. The tattered flags behind them belonged to the 5th Georgia and Cobb's Legion. (*Confederate Veteran*, 1897.)

In 1898, Atlanta was chosen as the site of the 8th National United Confederate Veterans Reunion to be held on July 20, 1898. Georgia hosted four national reunions, with Atlanta again hosting it on September 6, 1919, and October 14, 1941. Macon hosted in 1912. This image features the Atlanta Reunion Executive Committee. Gen. Clement A. Evans, who served as president, can be seen in the middle of the third row. Many of Atlanta's leading citizens are in the photo. For additional information concerning Gen. C. A. Evans, see page 87. (*Confederate Veteran*, 1898.)

Veterans and Daughters of the Confederacy gather at the courthouse in Decatur, Georgia, in January 1898 to aid and plan for the Atlanta reunion in July. The courthouse in the background was later replaced with a larger building. The columns were donated to a Confederate monument to be erected on the courthouse square. It is unknown if any of the column material was used, but an obelisk was dedicated in 1908. (*Confederate Veteran*, 1898.)

Veterans march down one of the city streets in Atlanta during the National United Confederate Veterans Reunion in July 1898. Both black and white children can be seen walking with the old veterans next to the many trolley car tracks. The Columbia Theatre can be seen in the distance next to the old Atlanta City Hall. The Henry Grady Monument was placed in front of city hall in 1891. (Courtesy of Kenan Research Center at Atlanta History Center.)

The 10th Georgia Infantry is pictured at the 1898 Atlanta reunion. They are from left to right as follows: (first row) I. A. Thompson, D. McDuffie, C. W. Horton, J. C. Hill, D. I. Walden, J. L. Maddox, Miss E. V. McLaws, John Harris, J. J. Camp, R. R. Horton, M. A. Camp, W. W. Hudson, D. A. Ray, R. B. McBride, E. A. Brown, and A. J. McBride Jr.; (second row) unidentified, Maj. P. H. Loud, James E. Hudson, H. Sturges, H. S. Dibble, unidentified, W. L. Camp, J. X. Beauchamp, J. S. Alford, J. M. Dorsey, Henry Rivers, J. W. Horton, W. D. Strickland, and A. J. McBride. (Courtesy of John W. Lynch.)

The "Dixie Boys" were Company A, 57th Georgia Infantry, from Thomas County. This reunion image taken around 1900 features veterans Judge Bibb, J. O. J. Lewis, J. C. Stanaland, A. B. Cone, Judge W. H. Bibb, P. S. Rainey, Redden Smith Sr., T. J. Humpreys, William Smith, Joel Culpepper, Jasper Miles, Sidney Williams, Nathaniel Brown, Jim Smith, and W. T. Beasley. (Courtesy of Bessie Hopkins Collection, Thomas County Historical Society.)

Jimmerson S. Alford poses in his reunion uniform. He enlisted as a private in Company E, 2nd Georgia Regiment, 1st Georgia Reserves, in September 1863 in Fayette County, Georgia. Born on June 6, 1818, in Fayette County, he was married first to Susan Morris and then to Sarah Brassell. He died on March 22, 1902, and is buried in the Alford/Brassell Cemetery in South Fayette County. (Courtesy of Fayette County Historical Society.)

Pictured c. 1900 is the Old Soldiers Day, held in Tyrone, Georgia. The annual reunion was always held on the third Friday in July and lasted into the 1960s with descendants. Thomas N. Farr is standing on the far left, Dan Banks is sixth from the left, and Edward C. Stephens is seventh from the left. Thomas Holt is in the front row kneeling, and Tom J. Askew is in the back center. (Courtesy of John W. Lynch.)

Thomas N. Farr was born in Fayette County, Georgia, on July 19, 1843. He enlisted on March 4, 1862, as a private in Company G, "Huie Guards," 44th Georgia Infantry. He was wounded in the left knee at Winchester, Virginia, on September 19, 1864, and captured at a hospital at Richmond, Virginia. After the war, he was a member of the Paul J. Semmes UCV Camp in Fayetteville and served for many years as the president of the Old Soldiers Reunion at Tyrone. He died on December 4, 1919, and is buried at Hopewell Methodist Church Cemetery in Tyrone. (Courtesy of John W. Lynch.)

Members of Company D, 27th Georgia Infantry, reunited in Gainesville, Georgia, c. 1900. Company D, which consisted of men from Hall County, Georgia, started at "half strength," enrolling only 428 men. It lost almost 40 percent of the 392 engaged at Seven Pines, while 85 men were killed or wounded at Gaines' Mill, 104 during the Maryland Campaign, 31 at Chancellorsville, and 74 at Olustee, Florida. The 27th surrendered at Bentonville, North Carolina, with General Johnston. (Courtesy of Mike Couch, SCV Camp 1404.)

This photograph shows aging members of the Confederate Veteran Association, Camp No. 756, U.C.V., Savannah, Georgia. Pictured from left to right are (first row) John Peterson; M. B. Garnett; Sgt. James Leonard; William Harden, commander of Camp 756; Gen. E. J. Thomas, commander of South Georgia Brigade; W. H. Mendal; and W. J. Torrance; (second row) J. T. Williams; William B. Puder; H. C. Hardy; J. P. Hardy; F. M. Hamlin of Virginia; Maj. R. J. Stewart; H. F. Douglas; and F. J. Chapman. Several pictured were Savannah Cadets, a company of boys, most of whom were about 16 years of age in 1861. (Courtesy of Joe Dawson.)

The Georgia Convention of the United Daughters of the Confederacy (UDC) was held at LaGrange, Georgia, in 1902. The image features a number of the participants, and of particular interest is the picture of the Winnie Davis Memorial, located in Athens, Georgia. The UDC had donated $25,000 for the construction of the memorial, named for the daughter of Jefferson Davis, who had been born in the Confederate White House in 1864. The building was constructed to provide housing for daughters of Confederate veterans who attended the State Normal School in Athens. (*Confederate Veteran*, 1902.)

Morgan County Confederate Veterans are posed for this image on June 1, 1903. On the lowest step is William Henry Elisha Harper (1840–1904) who served in Company A, "Thomasville Guards," 29th Georgia. On the back row, seated fifth from the left, is his brother Cordy T. Harper (1844–1917), who served in Company I, "Morgan and Henry Volunteers," 44th Georgia. The brothers were both born in Rutledge, Georgia, and both were wounded during the war. (Courtesy of Carolyn Lee Harper Johnson, great-granddaughter of W. H. E. Harper.)

The original Confederate Soldiers Home of Georgia, "the House that Grady Built," was completed in 1891 but was unoccupied by veterans until June 1901. In September of the same year, the building was destroyed by fire. The Colonial-style brick building pictured was opened in October 1902. After the old veterans were gone, the building served for a short time as a home for Confederate widows but was razed in 1967. For researchers, an index of soldiers at the home authored by Mike Brubaker is in the fall 2004 issue of *Georgia Genealogical Society Quarterly*.

Three unidentified Confederate Veterans are on the steps of Georgia's Confederate Soldiers Home in Atlanta. Pvt. Mendel Levey of the 59th Georgia was the first admitted in June 1901, dying one month after his entry. Over 1,000 veterans spent time at the home. Georgia was one of the leading states of the Confederacy in helping its soldiers and their widows with pensions after the war. This image has been restored. (Courtesy of Special Collections Department, Georgia State University Library.)

Standing on the steps of the Colquitt County Courthouse in Moultrie are some Confederate veterans living in the county. The picture was made on Confederate Memorial Day, April 26, 1903. Seventy-five veterans were present that day to receive their Cross of Honor from the Moultrie Chapter of the UDC. Another 22 were living in the county and could not be present that day. (Courtesy of Museum of Colquitt County History, Jack Bridwell, executive director.)

Born on April 15, 1836, in Henry County, William Allen Fuller began working for the Western and Atlantic Railroad in 1855. On April 12, 1862, he was the railroad engineer that pursued and recaptured the war-engine *General* that had been seized by 22 federal soldiers in civilian disguise. It became known as the "Andrews Raid," and a Disney movie, *The Great Locomotive Chase*, brought attention to the story. Gov. Joseph E. Brown commissioned him as captain in the Independent State Railroad Guards. This image is from 1904; he died on December 28, 1905, and is buried in Atlanta's Oakland Cemetery. (*The Historic "General,"* 1904.)

Members of the Cherokee Artillery, "Corput's Battery," pose at the state reunion in Rome, Georgia, September 14–15, 1904. Pictured are the following: (first row) Robert M. Stephens and Angus Laister; (second row) William B. Chapman, William P. Frix, Elizur N. McCurry, John C. Martin, R. Marion Mathis, and John T. Brown; (third row) James F. Russell, John W. Bowling, Joseph H. L. Duke, Wesley O. Connor, William C. New, Benjamin F. Frix, and Charles W. Gattis; (fourth row) James R. Scott, Lt. M. L. McWhorter, E. Mitchell Johnson, and John R. Kerr.

Like hundreds of ceremonies across Georgia, Confederate Memorial Day became synonymous with parades, celebrations, and remembering comrades. The picture on the left shows Carrollton veterans walking through the square in parade formation to the tune of "Dixie" and other favorites on Memorial Day, April 26, 1906. Ladies of the UDC, students, and children followed them. The image on the right shows their destination, the Carrollton City Cemetery, where the fallen were honored. Of course, a meal was to follow! (Courtesy of Susan Patton Hamersky.)

In 1905, the Georgia Division of the UDC voted to erect a monument in honor of Capt. Henry Wirz, the commandant of Andersonville Prison who had been executed by hanging by the U.S. government in 1865. Captain Wirz spurned an offer of his life in exchange for incriminating Jefferson Davis. Davis wrote in 1890, "He died a martyr to a cause through adherence to truth." The image shows UDC leaders at the dedication of the monument on May 12, 1909, in Andersonville. See page 52. (Courtesy of Peggy Sheppard, author of *Andersonville, Georgia, U.S.A.*)

A reunion of Company D, "Senoia Infantry," 19th Georgia Infantry, met on July 28, 1909, in Hollonville, Georgia. Present, from left to right, were the following: (first row) E. T. Peak, W. M. Odom, Hon. J. J. Flynt, Hon. E. M. Owen, C. T. Digby, and Hon. Abe Steinheimer; (second row) J. C. Elmore, T. H. Carlton, W. H. Summers, J. D. Johnson, Josephus Coggins, J. D. Garrison, A. O. Gay, Sydney Gay, G. W. Evan(s), Wm. Anderson, and J. C. McGahee. (Courtesy of John W. Lynch.)

A group of Confederate veterans met at the Fayette County Courthouse on Confederate Memorial Day, April 26, 1909. Daniel McLucas holds the flag and is fifth from the left on the back row. Joseph N. Banks is kneeling directly in front of him. Dan Banks is seventh from the left on the back row. The young ladies or "maids of honor" have memorial wreaths and refreshments. (Courtesy of John W. Lynch.)

The Upson County Confederate monument in Thomaston was dedicated on May 2, 1908, at the courthouse. Located on one side of the monument is "In Memory of the Confederate Soldiers of Upson" and on another is "Lest We Forget." A large group of veterans are at its base either on the dedication date or later. The courthouse features two other monuments, the first cannonball fired in the war and a sundial in honor of Gen. John B. Gordon. (Courtesy of John W. Lynch.)

Members of Sumter County United Confederate Veterans Camp posed on April 26, 1909, on the courthouse steps in Americus. Pictured from left to right are the following: (first row) J. H. Daniel, J. Z. Carey, H. D. Watts, T. E. Joiner, ? Gates, G. B. Suggs, James Alexander, J. D. Nicholson, J. Stafford Stephens, James M. Hansford, John Statum, and ? Toole; (second row) T. J. Singletary, P. R. Stanfield, Thomas J. Morgan, J. A. Wilson, Comdr. H. T. Davenport, color bearer Clinton Bray, P. H. Williams, Robert Arrington, William E. Felts, J. S. Bolton, Roland Cheek, W. P. Persons, James H. Rogers, ? Williams, Henry Mashburn, J. P. Britton, J. P. Mask, Charles Williams, and William S. Moore. (Courtesy of Alexander H. Stephens Camp, PO Box 126, Americus, Georgia 31709; copies are available.)

A group of Confederate veterans and young "maids of honor" can be seen at a reunion of veterans in Adairsville, Georgia, c. 1910. They are posed in front of the Adairsville Methodist Church. Adairsville was the site of several events during the war: the last leg of the "Great Locomotive Chase" occurred at the Adairsville Depot in 1862, the Georgia State Arsenal located there was destroyed in 1864 in Sherman's March, and it is the home of Barnsley Garden ruins. (Courtesy of the Bartow History Center, Cartersville, Georgia.)

Hundreds of soldiers answered the call to service from DeKalb County. This c. 1910 image shows a group of United Confederate Veterans in DeKalb County, Georgia. Confederate groups like the one pictured here met in the basement of the old courthouse until 1916. Note the veterans wearing reunion badges, which are widely collected as treasures today. A camp banner is in the background but is pointed in the wrong direction for the image. (Courtesy of Photographic Collection, DeKalb History Center.)

Clement Anselm Evans was born in Stewart County on February 25, 1833. Enlisting as a private in Company E, "Bartow Guards," 31st Georgia, he rose quickly through the ranks, becoming a major in 1861 and a colonel in 1862, leading the regiment at Fredericksburg. He was appointed brigadier general on May 19, 1864. He was wounded five times, twice severely, and became a division commander of 2nd Corps, Army of Northern Virginia. After becoming a renowned Methodist minister after the war, he was active in reunions and the UCV, serving as commander-in-chief. He edited and contributed to the 12-volume *Confederate Military History*. He died in Atlanta on July 2, 1911, and is buried at Oakland Cemetery.

GENERAL CLEMENT A. EVANS,
EMINENT CARDINAL COLUMBIAN WOODMEN.
RENOWNED CONFEDERATE GENERAL
/v CHIEF OF STAFF TO GOVERNOR HOKE SMITH · LEADING THE INAUGURAL
PROCESSION·IN FRONT OF THE COLUMBIAN WOODMEN BUILDING·PEACHTREE ST. ATLANTA·GA.

State veterans met in Rome, Georgia, in 1911. Robert Borders Everett drives the lead car, and it is believed that Nathan Bedford Forrest Jr., General Forrest's son, is on the passenger side. The driver's father, Robert Williams Everett of Polk County, rides in the back seat, far right. R. W. Everett was born in Houston County, Georgia, in 1839 and had served in Forrest's command. Living in Rockmart, he served several terms in the state legislature and in 1891 was elected to the U.S. Congress. He died in 1915 and is buried in Cedartown's Greenwood Cemetery.

Over 100 members of Camp #1227 of the Confederate Veterans of Bulloch County pose at their annual reunion on July 19, 1911, in front of the Jaeckel Hotel in Statesboro. More than 2,000 people attended the event. The hotel still stands and is on the National Register of Historic Places. Miss Inez Williams, sponsor of the camp, can be seen in the middle next to color bearer T. J. Whitaker. (Courtesy of Robert Alderman of Columbus; Smith Callaway Banks, official historian of Bulloch County; and Henderson Library, Georgia Southern University.)

On the 50th anniversary of their departure from Augusta, Georgia, for Virginia, members of the "West Point Guards," Company D, 4th Georgia Infantry, from Troup County, posed for this photo on May 4, 1911. Shown here from left to right are (seated) D. O. Robinson, Dr. B.G. Poer, Col. William W. Hulbert, and S. M. Wallace; (standing) T. W. Johnson, L. T. C. Lovelace, J. S. Baker, Ansel Sterne, and W. A. Harwell. (Courtesy of Troup County Archives.)

Confederate Veterans gathered around the new Confederate monument on April 26, 1911, at the Jefferson City Square for its dedication. The Jefferson Chapter of the United Daughters of the Confederacy erected the monument in honor of the veterans. "Lest we forget" is inscribed on one side and "Comrades" on another. The original monument featured a Confederate soldier at the top; however, in 1940, the soldier was accidentally toppled, and a cross of honor was later added. (Courtesy of Jackson County Historical Society.)

A rare postcard published by the J. W. Burke Company of Macon declares "Greetings of Macon GA to the U.S.C.V., May 7th, 8th & 9th, 1912." The card features a number of special images: a portrait of Pres. Jefferson Davis, the Confederate monument of Macon with wreath, the Macon monument to the women of the Confederacy, the different flags of the Confederacy, an American eagle, and a poem to the fallen.

This panoramic view by Pattons Studio shows the tent city located at the racetrack in Central City Park in Macon, Georgia. The tent city housed the many veterans who were to make Macon the darling of the Confederacy from May 5 through May 7, 1912. The camp had been arranged with military precision and accommodated 7,000. Named for General Gordon, the camp featured 26 streets, named for Southern generals, Southern states, and the host city. The Macon Hussars provided the guarding of the camp. Information about the Macon Reunion came from the

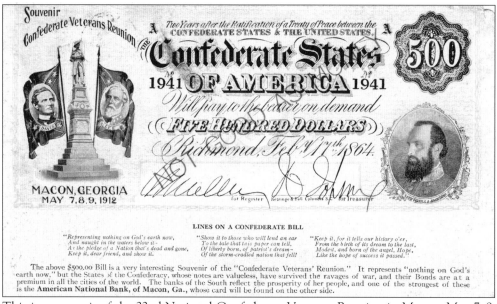

This is a souvenir of the 22nd National Confederate Veterans Reunion in Macon, May 7–9, 1912. This oversized postcard was released by the American National Bank of Macon, Georgia, to promote business and welcome the visitors to Macon. The card features a $500 Confederate bill with the image of Lt. Gen. Thomas J. "Stonewall" Jackson. On the left is the impressive Macon monument dedicated to men of Bibb County surrounded by Confederate battle flags with portraits of Jefferson Davis and Robert E. Lee.

Macon Telegraph. In the photograph, the crowd has gathered for opening ceremonies and the raising of the flag. Numerous buggies and autos surround the track. Jackson, Lee, and Longstreet Avenues can be seen. The first night saw 4,000 veterans. The first meal featured a supper of steak, scrambled eggs, boiled potatoes, applesauce, cake, bread and butter, coffee, and other "fixings." As one veteran of reunions declared, "No other city we have visited has so well prepared for us!" Another tent city at the half-mile racetrack housed the Sons of Veterans.

QUEEN AND HER MAIDS OF THE CONFEDERATE VETERANS REUNION, MAY 7-8-9, MACON, GA

On May 8, 1912, Mary Scandrett was crowned the Queen of the Reunion. Driving up Coleman Hill in Macon, her carriage was led by eight white horses. The honorary escort was provided by the Thomas Hardeman Camp of Sons of Veterans and the 2nd Regiment comprised the formal escort. Ms. Scandrett wore a white satin dress draped in Venetian lace. She wore a crown of red and white and was given a diamond ring for winning the competition. The postcard image was by Geo. S. Riley Jr.

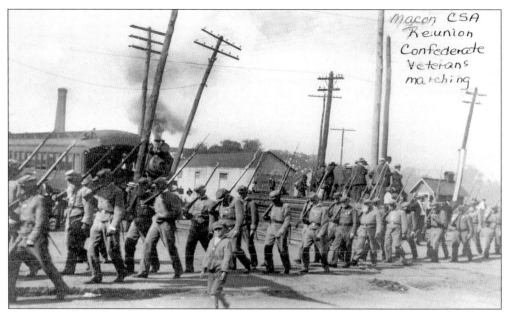

The *Macon Telegraph* was quoted as saying to the veterans, "Macon is today the Mecca of those who remain of the thinning gray line that followed the Southern Cross. Here they meet again around the camp fires to recount their experiences in the days that tried men's souls—to drink once more from the same canteen—and to talk of those that have gone before to Fame's Eternal Camping Ground." The men lined up for the parade in the Central Park and from beginning to end took an hour and 25 minutes.

Yet another greeting from the *Macon Telegraph* reads, "Bless and welcome the heroes that are without proximate rivals in the annals of war; men who, overpowered by vastly superior numbers, turned the ashes of defeat into victories of peace, and builded [*sic*] within their own time and generation a Southern empire superior in greatness and prosperity to the combined North and South of the Sixties."

The parade was led by the marshal of the parade, followed by a band and the veterans, who included both mounted and foot units. The mounted units included Forrest's, Wheeler's, and the Georgia cavalry. General officers and their staffs were also often mounted. Gov. Joseph M. Brown, wartime governor Joseph E. Brown's son, and other dignitaries had a viewing stand at the corner of Cherry and Third Streets.

The units on foot were arranged in this order: Army of Northern Virginia Department, the Army of Tennessee Department, and the Army of Trans-Mississippi Department. In total, over 6,000 veterans participated in the parade. The day of the parade was a very hot sunny day, and Macon citizens gave the old veterans water along the way. It was remarkable for men mostly in their sixties and seventies.

Following the infantry units were the Association of Army and Navy Medical officers, another band, and then Confederate Navy veterans. Leaders of the Southern Memorial Association, more than 100 girls of the Milledgeville's Normal and Industrial College, the Dublin Boy Scouts (who walked 50 miles to Macon to participate), and countless vehicles were also involved.

This view shows several of the vehicles in the parade. The third vehicle, an "auto truck," carried a dozen veterans with a banner, "The Immortal 600." On August 20, 1864, a group of 600 Confederate officers—including 58 from Georgia—were placed in a stockade in front of Union batteries at the siege of Charleston. After 45 days under "friendly" fire, they were moved to Fort Pulaski, Georgia, where a number died due to horrendous conditions. These men became famous for their plight and were evermore known in the South as "The Immortal 600."

This postcard image shows the queen's float in the Macon Reunion Parade. The float was drawn through the streets by a team of white horses. The queen was seated on the float, and the maids, wearing white dresses and hats and carrying American Beauty roses, stood around the edge. They were greeted enthusiastically by the crowds.

The queen and her court were Queen Mary Scandrett, Pearl Lewis of Valdosta, Mattie Lews Dodson of Americus, Agnes Jones of Albany, Harriet Calhoun of Atlanta, Lucy Eve Allen of Augusta, Susan Grantland of Griffin, Mildred Moultrie of Rome, Elizabeth Kyle of Columbus, LaLage Darwin of Athens, and Mattie Chappell, Lucille Turner, Jennie Riley, and Jewel Jacobs of Macon.

Warren A. Mosley is featured in this photograph by F. Bernd at the Macon Reunion of 1912. He enlisted as a private on August 5, 1861, in Company H, "Baldwin Blues," 4th Georgia Infantry. He was wounded and captured at Strasburg, Virginia, in 1862, exchanged, and wounded at Chancellorsville in May 1863. In April, he was elected to captain of the 4th Regiment Georgia Reserve Cavalry and surrendered at Milledgeville in 1865. After the war, he served many years as a Macon policeman. Note the veteran in front of the streetcar with the wooden leg.

A group of veterans gathered in Macon at the Confederate Veterans Reunion, May 7–9, 1912, standing in front of Macon's monument to the women of the Confederacy. From left to right are (seated) Jim Johnson, Hiram Vauzort, Jim Sexton, Clem Duncan, Mr. ? Harden, John Jesup, and Andrew Wilson; (standing) Mr. ? Sammons, Jack Womack, Mrs. Anna B. Love, Joe Henderson, Jack Green Braswell, C. B. Herb, J. M. Britt, James Anderson, Mrs. K. Dunlop, and Gus Daily. (Courtesy of Middle Georgia Archives, Washington Memorial Library, Macon.)

Hardy Beacham Smith was born in the Anderson community of Laurens County, Georgia, on October 24, 1841. He enlisted in Company H, "Blackshear Guards," 14th Georgia Infantry, and was elected first sergeant and then junior second lieutenant. Wounded at the Battle of Mechanicsville, he had to have his right arm amputated. He was elected captain on September 17, 1863. Returning to Georgia in 1864, he served as the 5th District enrolling officer. He died on December 6, 1912, and is buried in Northview Cemetery. He was very active in UCV, serving as Eastern Georgia Division Commander. His Confederate Cross of Honor is proudly displayed on his uniform. (Courtesy of Laurens County Historical Society.)

A group of veterans wait at the East Rome Depot in Rome, Georgia, in May 1913 to attend the Confederate Reunion in Chattanooga, Tennessee. From left to right are (kneeling) Andy W. Hicks and Capt. John Duke; (standing) Capt. James H. May, Steve Eberhart, ? Selman, James H. L. Duke, Capt. S. C. Lindsey, George C. Wyatt, ? Archer, Richard Dean Price, Capt. John J. Seay, George Hillman Braden, and Dr. Daniel T. McCall. Steve Eberhart, a former slave and Confederate veteran, was a fixture at many of the reunions. (Courtesy of Rome Area History Museum.)

John O. Waddell was born in Greene County, Georgia, on December 3, 1841. He moved to Cedartown in 1854 and was appointed corporal and then sergeant in the Troop Artillery. He was wounded and captured at Crampton's Gap, Maryland, in 1862. Later released, he was wounded at Chancellorsville. He was appointed first lieutenant and then adjutant of 20th Georgia Infantry in 1863. He again suffered wounds at Chickamauga and at the Wilderness. After the war, he became Georgia's first assistant commissioner of agriculture, secretary of the Confederate Memorial Board, and commander of Georgia Division, UCV. He died in 1913 and is buried in the Greenwood Cemetery in Cedartown. (*Confederate Veteran*, 1914.)

Veterans of Company F, "Johnson Greys," 14th Georgia Infantry of Thomas Brigade, A. P. Hill's Corp, Army of Northern Virginia, gather at the train station in Vidalia, Georgia. They are journeying to the 50th anniversary of Gettysburg, July 1–3, 1913. Henry Jasper Kight is sitting second from the left on the front row. At war's end, 14 members of the company surrendered at Appomattox. (Courtesy of Thad and Brian Beckum, great-great-grandsons of Kight.)

Confederate veterans are aligned for review for the Confederate Memorial Day parade on April 26, 1913, in LaGrange, Georgia. (Courtesy of Troup County Archives.)

Confederate Memorial Day, *c.* 1915, was celebrated in a parade on West Park Square in Marietta, Georgia. The procession is led by a cavalry unit of veterans followed by the veterans of the infantry. (Courtesy of the Marietta Museum.)

The Georgia Division UCV's 18th annual reunion was hosted in Americus, Georgia, on August 24–25, 1916. It took place in the Rylander Warehouse, which today serves as the headquarters for Habitat for Humanity, Inc. Over 700 veterans were entertained at the Windsor Hotel, given passes to the theatre and ball games, and received all the Chero-Cola they could drink. The photograph shows the grand parade through the streets that were draped with Confederate flags and images. (Courtesy of Alexander H. Stephens Camp #78 and John Carroll.)

Confederate veterans of Company K, 34th Georgia, from Carroll and Heard met on July 18, 1917, at the home of Mr. P. P. Staples of Roopville, Georgia. Present that day were four veterans of the company and nine guests from other companies. The veterans present were W. L. Craven, age 82; G. W. Story, 77; F. M. Screws, 76; J. A. McDonald, 70; Judge J. T. Norman, 70; D. W. Stallings, 83; Jonathan Copeland, 80; G. F. Cheney, 73; J. J. Walker, 75; Rev. W. W. Roop, 76; T. J. Jackson, 76; W. B. Stevens, 71 (seventh from the left); and W. O. Perry, 72. (Courtesy of Troup County Archives.)

Veterans of Thomas County pose for this photo about 1918. They include, from left to right, (first row) unidentified, Leon Neel, John Dekle, William M. Jones, P. S. Heeth, and James Jones; (second row) unidentified, D. H. Parker, unidentified, T. L. Wyche, unidentified, William Vonier, and two unidentified. (Courtesy of Thomas County Historical Society, Thomasville, Georgia.)

Bill Yopp, drummer, and his former master, Capt. T. M. Yopp, were members of Company H, "Blackshear Guards," 14th Georgia Infantry. After the war, Bill was a free man but chose to work on the Yopp plantation until 1870. Working in a number of jobs all over the world, he returned to Georgia to find his former master prepared to enter the Confederate Soldier's Home in Atlanta. Bill raised money for the veterans and later lived in the home. He is buried with his comrades in the Confederate Cemetery in Marietta. (Courtesy of Laurens County Historical Society.)

Confederate veterans pose at Troup County Courthouse on April 26, 1919. They are, from left to right, (first row) Cmdr. J. F. Edwards and Adj. J. B. Strong; (second row) N. H. Sledge, M. M. Sledge, F. M. Longley, W. C. Cox, R. F. Candle, J. D. Hunter, T. White, A. J. Fuller, L. R. Greer, J. C. Freeman, T. J. Harwell, J. Q. Burton, J. Hightower, and M. Thrailkill; (third row) unidentified, H. H. Towns, R. M. Stinson, W. W. Covin, W. W. Turner, J. D. Tharp, W. V. Gray, J. A. Christopher, ? Gaines, H. W. Haralson, A. J. Dainel, A. C. Hudson, S. W. Smithwick, O. D. Hardy, J. T. Willingham, W. E. Brady, T. J. Teaver, and ? Kennedy. (Courtesy of Troup Archives.)

WELCOME U. C. V.!
TWENTY-NINTH ANNUAL REUNION.
UNITED CONFEDERATE VETERANS.
ATLANTA, GA., OCTOBER 7 TO 11 1919
Above composite picture including actual aerial photograph of Atlanta, designed and copyrighted by The Atlanta Journal Staff Photographers.

A postcard featuring a flower of the South greets veterans and visitors to the Twenty-ninth National Annual Reunion of the United Confederate Veterans, held in Atlanta on October 7–11, 1919. The image features a young maiden draped in a hallowed flag offering the veterans the key to the city and Atlanta's hospitality. The foreground features an aerial view of Atlanta from 1919 and was designed by the staff of the *Atlanta Journal-Constitution*.

Abel Marion Crow was born August 18, 1844, in Crow Valley near Dalton. Abel was attending Georgia Military Institute in Marietta when war broke out. He enlisted in the Macon Light Artillery and hid under a cannon's tarp on a flatcar when it went through Dalton so his parents would not see that he had joined. Returning home after the war, he was involved in the murder of a "scalawag." Leaving Georgia, he drifted around Texas before settling in the Chickasaw Nation, Indian Territory, in Oklahoma. He was very active in Confederate reunions. He died on May 3, 1927, and is buried in Rosedale Cemetery in Ada, Oklahoma. (Courtesy of Janet Compere Rhodes, great-granddaughter of Abel.)

A group of veterans poses for this image by W. M. Boynton in downtown Carrollton. They are, from left to right, (first row) unidentified, W. M. Spivey, W. B. Stevens, Howard Pitts, Charles Bloodworth, John Bowen, George Lyle, two unidentified, James Bryce, and John Mullinax; (second row) unidentified, Thomas Jackson, George W. Harper, three unidentified, W. O. Perry, Ashley Nelson, Henry C. Reeves, two unidentified, James Kuglar, unidentified, George Cheney (flag holder), unidentified, and J. T. Norman. A slightly different pose of the same individuals can be found at the Troup Archives. (Courtesy of Forrest's Escort and McDaniel-Curtis SCV Camps.)

This postcard view shows a Confederate Memorial Day Parade in Augusta, Georgia, c. 1920. The route of the parade took the "Old Guard" down Broad Street, past the Augusta Confederate monument, on their way to Magnolia Cemetery to hear speeches and for the laying of flowers. Georgia Confederate generals E. P. Alexander, Goode Bryan, V. J. B. Girardey, J. K. Jackson, W. D. Smith, M. A. Stovall, and A. R. Wright are buried there. Note the three-story Confederate flag. See page 121.

In commemoration of Memorial Day, a reunion was held in Rockmart, Georgia, c. 1922. Veterans here are on the front steps of what was then Rockmart City Hall. W. M. Trippe sits in the middle of the front row holding a cane between his legs. "Wild Bill" Camp is the last seated individual on the first row. Others present that day included Roe Lee, Tom Morris, Mr. ? Watts, George Morgan, John Dunn, Preacher ? Head, Jack Whitehead, and Dave Browning.

Veterans march two by two up Broad Street in Thomasville, Georgia. The reunion was held in October 1924. The street is adorned with both U.S. and Confederate flags. Although Thomas County did not see a battle on their soil, they sent about 1,500 men to fight for the Confederacy. (Courtesy of the Hansell Watt Collection, Thomas County Historical Society, Thomasville, Georgia.)

These veterans gathered at the Thomas County Courthouse lawn after the parade in 1924. After every good reunion parade or memorial exercise, the veterans gathered for a meal. Comrades shared memories of battles long ago and of those who were departed, as well as talk of their children and grandchildren, the crops, the politics, and of course the weather. Often, a reunion would later be remembered for how well the men were received and how good the food was. (Courtesy of the Hansell Watt Collection, Thomas County Historical Society, Thomasville, Georgia.)

These Confederate veterans were still prepared to defend their homes and state. Their numbers dwindling, these Carroll County veterans were featured in the 1927 centennial parade for Carrollton, Georgia. The photograph was from the B. M. Long album, courtesy of Aubrey Jones. It was featured in *At Home in Carrollton 1827–1994* by Dr. Ben Griffith and published by the Carroll County Historical Society. (Courtesy of Special Collections, Myron House, University of West Georgia, Carrollton.)

This image, used on the cover, shows the unveiling and dedication photograph of the Confederate monument in Watkinsville, Georgia, in April 1927 at the Watkinsville City Park. The children are contributor Roy Ward and Dorothy Harris. Also pictured, from left to right, are (second row) Barry A. Maxey, William F. Phillips, J. M. McLeroy, J. G. Hansford, J. F. Osborne, and W. H. Anderson; (third row) Annie Johnston, Robert B. Harris, local UDC president Florine Meaders, Lucy Wilson, and James L. Miller. The monument today is located on the courthouse lawn in Watkinsville. (Courtesy of Dr. Roy Ward, Watkinsville.)

A very large group of Georgia and Florida veterans gathered at a reunion in Thomasville, Georgia, c. 1930. The first flag to the right of the entrance belonged to the North Georgia Brigade of the UCV. The image was cropped and has many more veterans in the original. (Courtesy of State of Florida Archives.)

Pictured here in front of the flag of the North Georgia Brigade are, from left to right, Sarah Hardy, Sarah Daniel, Dr. Charles Kennon Henderson Sr. (1846–1937), Virginia Colquitt, and Kate Daniel. The others are unidentified. The photograph was taken at a Confederate reunion in Thomaston on September 24, 1930. Dr. Henderson served in Company F, 3rd Georgia. He was a renowned Baptist minister and historian, and he served as chaplain and commander of the North Georgia Brigade, UCV. He was a leading citizen in Polk, Carroll, and every county he served. His likeness appears as one of the soldiers at the Cyclorama. He donated the flag to the A. H. Stephens Park Museum, where it is on display. Contributor Susan Patton Hamersky is his great-granddaughter.

One of Georgia's most unique Confederate monuments, at Redwine Methodist Church near Gainesville, no longer exists. Ernest and Velvia Laws stand beside a 61-and-a-quarter-foot-tall totem pole that honored the service of the veterans of Company D, 27th Georgia. Dedicated in July 1936, the monument was created by Roy Ledford of Gainesville and painted by H. R. McBride of Indiana. The monument featured a roster of the company, various events, and war personalities. W. T. "Wash" Gaines, the only surviving member of the company, was present. Richard B. Russell Jr. was the primary speaker. (Courtesy of Mike Couch, SCV Camp #1404.)

This photograph shows the shrinking number of Confederate veterans able to celebrate. These veterans and their escorts are at the Confederate Veteran's Parade in Atlanta, Georgia, in 1939. This image is featured on a 1939 first-day cover postal issue proclaiming the same. (Courtesy of Special Collections Department, Georgia State University Library.)

A rare five-generation photograph features the Kight and Beckum families. Seated in the center is patriarch Henry Jasper Kight, who served in Company F, "Johnson Greys," 14th Georgia. To his left is son Henry Lee Kight, and to his right is grandson Luther Kight. Standing are great-grandson Alfred Paul Beckum (holding great-great-grandson Alfred Paul Beckum Jr.) and great-grandson Thomas Henry Beckum with great-great-grandson H. G. Beckum. Henry had just returned from the 75th anniversary reunion of Gettysburg in 1937. He lived until 1942. (Courtesy of Thad and Brian Beckum, great-great-grandsons of Henry Jasper Kight.)

On April 26, 1941, a monument in Commerce, Georgia, was dedicated to the women and veterans of the War Between the States in Spencer Park. The J. E. B. Stuart Chapter of the UDC had long wished to erect and dedicate a memorial. Miss Corrinne Harden and Charles W. O'Rear Jr., pictured here, unveiled the monument. High school students sang "Dixie," and wreaths for the veterans, the women of the 1860s, and for deceased daughters were placed at the base of the monument. (Courtesy of Jackson County Historical Society.)

Lest You Forget was a photocard sent from 1943 to 1944 to chapters of the UDC as a reminder of those who remained in Georgia's Confederate Soldier's Home. Pictured from left to right are (seated) Col. C. M. Dupree, born 1846 in Marion County; Col. L. J. Snellgrove, born in Sumter County in 1846; registered nurse Mary D. Goudelock; and J. T. Pittman, born in Cherokee County (Georgia or Alabama) in 1848; (standing) Maj. Gen. H. T. Dowling, commander of the Georgia Division, born in 1849 in Lowndes County; and Gen. J. R. Jones, past commander, born in Taliaferro County in 1845.

With time, the ranks of Georgia's "Old Guard" dwindled until there was but one. Born in Georgia on July 10, 1845, Gen. William Joshua Bush became Georgia's last living Confederate veteran. At age 16, he enlisted as a private into Company B, "Ramah Guards" of Wilkinson County, 14th Georgia Infantry, in July 1861. He died at the age of 107 years old on November 11, 1952, and is buried in Fitzgerald, Georgia, at the Evergreen Cemetery. The Blue and Gray Museum in Fitzgerald features artifacts owned by the general and is well worth visiting. (Courtesy of Special Collections Department, Georgia State University Library.)

Three

A FEW HONORED CONFEDERATES IN BRONZE AND STONE

Originally located in Chippewa Square, Savannah (seen here), were the busts of Gen. Francis Stebbins Bartow, born in Savannah, and Gen. Lafayette McLaws, born in Augusta but a resident of Savannah after the war. Bartow was a secessionist and attended the state convention. As a brigadier general, he was killed at the First Battle of Manassas in 1861. In his honor, Cass County was renamed Bartow County in 1861 (see page 8). McLaws became a major general on May 23, 1862, and had great military service, especially in his opposition to Sherman. Both are buried in Laurel Grove Cemetery in Savannah. The busts are now located in Forsyth Park next to the Confederate monument.

John Price Allen (1831–1905) served as captain of Company K, 7th Regiment Georgia State Troops, and was elected captain of Company H, 55th Georgia Infantry, on April 20, 1862. Captured at Cumberland Gap, Tennessee, in 1863, he became a member of the Immortal 600. The monument pictured honors him and other Allen family members at the place of his birth, Midville, Burke County, Georgia. The monument is located in front of the Midville United Methodist Church and was erected by Jerry A. Maddox. A dedication service was held in 1999 with church and SCV members participating. (Courtesy of Jerry A. Maddox, great-great-grandson of John.)

Born in South Carolina, Joseph Emerson Brown and family moved to Union County, Georgia, when he was 19. He studied law, was admitted to the Bar, and rose to be a judge. At age 36, he became governor of Georgia in 1857 and was Georgia's only Confederate governor. He was often at odds with Pres. Jefferson Davis over policy and the use of Georgia troops. He later served as a U.S. senator. The monument of him and his wife is located on the state capitol grounds, placed in 1928 and sculpted by I. D. Dumley and G. Morett. He died on November 30, 1894, and is buried in Atlanta's Oakland Cemetery (see page 2).

Jeff Davis County, Georgia, was created in 1905 from parts of Appling and Coffee Counties. The county was named for Jefferson Davis, president of the Confederacy. The bust monument pictured is in Hazelhurst, the county seat, and was erected by the Appling Grays, SCV Camp #918. Another bust can be found at the Jefferson Davis Memorial Site in Irwinville, Georgia, where he was captured at the end of the war. He spent two years in prison for treason but was released before a trial. He died in 1889 at the age of 81.

Maj. Charles A. Dunwoody (1829–1905) was a Confederate soldier and pioneer citizen of Dunwoody, Georgia, named for him. A nine-foot monument was dedicated to him on November 22, 2003, with about 100 people attending the service. The monument, located at the Ebenezer Primitive Baptist Church on Roberts Road in Dunwoody, was donated by Jerry A. Maddox, commander of the Maj. Charles A. Dunwoody SCV Camp #1682, Dunwoody. A group of Sons of Confederate Veterans stands in front of the monument with Commander Maddox kneeling in the foreground. (Courtesy of Jerry A. Maddox.)

Monument to General Nathan Bedford Forrest, Rome, Ga.

Gen. Nathan Bedford Forrest is considered by many to be the finest cavalry officer ever to serve in America. Born in Tennessee in 1821 and raising a battalion of mounted troops, he was quickly promoted, reaching the rank of major general on December 4, 1863, and lieutenant general on February 28, 1865. Feared by Union troops, he was credited with saving Rome, Georgia, from destruction. He died in 1877. A large monument was erected in his honor in downtown Rome and was later moved to Myrtle Hill Cemetery. The monument reads "Erected by N. B. Forrest Chapter, UDC, May 3, 1908."

The proclaimed youngest Confederate regular, David Bailey Freeman, served in Company D, 6th Georgia Cavalry. After the war, he became a newspaper publisher, editor, and writer. At different times, he was the mayor of Calhoun, Cedartown, and Cartersville. He later became general of the Northern Brigade, Georgia Division, UCV. He died on June 18, 1929, and is buried in Cartersville at Oak Hill Cemetery. This photograph by Leslie McCrary features Dennis Q. Venner portraying young David at his grave in "An Evening in Oak Hill Cemetery," presented by the Bartow History Center and the Pumphouse Players. See page 59. (Courtesy of Leslie McCrary and Dennis Q. Venner.)

The General John B. Gordon equestrian statue was unveiled on the grounds of the state capitol on May 25, 1907. The monument was sculpted by Solon H. Borglum, brother of Gutzon of Mount Rushmore fame. The horse represents Gordon's steed, Marye, which was captured from the Federals on Marye's Heights during the Second Battle of Fredricksburg. After the war, General Gordon returned to Georgia and became Georgia's most popular citizen. He was elected to the U.S. Senate three times and was governor of Georgia from 1886 to 1890. He died in 1904 and is buried in Atlanta at the Oakland Cemetery. Fort Gordon and Gordon College were named for him. Additional bronze plaques not pictured were later added to the base of the statue. See pages 53 and 72 for additional information.

GORDON MONUMENT, ATLANTA, GA.

After the war, having served Georgia as a Confederate senator, Benjamin Harvey Hill was elected to Congress in 1873 and to the U.S. Senate in 1873. He died on August 16, 1882. The statue to Benjamin H. Hill was dedicated on the state capitol grounds on May 1, 1886. Gov. John B. Gordon and Jefferson Davis were both present, and Henry Grady served as the master of ceremonies for the dedication. The statue, made of Italian marble, began to weather and was moved inside the capitol building, where it is located today. It was the work of Alexander Doyle. See page 2 for additional information.

Gen Joseph Eggleston Johnston (1807–1891), a Virginian, was the commander of the Army of Northern Virginia until wounded at Seven Pines and replaced by Gen. Robert E. Lee. Later given the command of the Army of Tennessee, he was responsible for the defense of Georgia during Sherman's march through Georgia. The men admired him, but Pres. Jefferson Davis replaced him with Gen. John B. Hood before the fall of Atlanta. The image above shows the dedication of the monument to General Johnston located in Dalton, Georgia. Miss Belle Kinney, the sculptor, can be seen standing to the left addressing the crowd. (*Confederate Veteran*, 1912.)

Gen. Robert E. Lee (1807–1872), a Virginian, is probably the most revered American soldier after George Washington. Serving as the commander of the Army of Northern Virginia, after Joseph E. Johnston was wounded at the Battle of Seven Pines, Lee became the Confederacy's best hope for military victory. Contending against a much larger force and lack of materials ultimately led to surrender. His example of conduct after the war made him a legend. He said, "Abandon your animosities and make your sons Americans." This equestrian statue of Lee and his horse Traveler is located in Gregory Park in Richmond Hill, Georgia. He also can be found on the Augusta and Hawkinsville, Georgia, monuments.

After the Second Battle of Manassas and Sharpsburg, Brig. Gen. James Longstreet was promoted to lieutenant general on October 9, 1862. General Longstreet was placed in command of the First Corps, Army of Northern Virginia, winning praise as a corps commander. His actions at Fredericksburg, Gettysburg, Chickamauga, and the Wilderness, where he was wounded, are legendary. The monument shown is located at his home site in Gainesville, Georgia. Dying on January 2, 1904, the last of the Confederate senior commanders, he is buried in Gainesville's Alta Cemetery. The base of the monument states that it was endowed by the Denton L. Hardaway Estate, designed and sculpted by Gregory Johnson, and erected in 2001 by James Longstreet Chapter #46 UDC (see page 52).

Gen. Leonidas Polk, born in North Carolina, graduated from West Point in 1827. A friend of Jefferson Davis at West Point, he resigned his commission and entered the Episcopal ministry, becoming a bishop. At the outbreak of war, he was appointed a major general and later lieutenant general, becoming a corps commander of the Army of Tennessee. While observing the federal position with Generals Hardee and Johnston on Pine Mountain near Marietta, he was killed by a cannon shot on June 14, 1864. The 20-foot monument was erected by J. Gid and Mary Morris on April 10, 1902, and marks the site of his death. Wartime illustrator Alfred Waud's pencil drawing of his death is in the background. Today the monument is on private property.

The head of the statue of Col. Christopher Columbus Sanders can be found today at the Northeast Georgia History Center in Gainesville, Georgia. Col. C. C. Sanders (1840–1908) served as a colonel in the 24th Georgia Infantry. The monument of Colonel Sanders, which was located on the corner of the U.S. Post Office, featured a statue of the colonel in a chair supported on eight-foot-high columns, seen in the image on the wall behind his head. The statue was toppled in the devastating tornado that hit Gainesville in 1936. The locals chuckle that it was the only Confederate monument ever allowed on federal property. (Courtesy of Northeast Georgia History Center.)

William Henry Talbot Walker was born November 26, 1816, in Augusta, Georgia. Graduating in 1837 from West Point, he distinguished himself in the Seminole and Mexican Wars, surviving critical wounds in both. Resigning his commission at the onset of war, he was appointed major general and then brigadier general. On May 23, 1863, he was promoted to major general and died on July 22, 1864, in the Battle of Atlanta. This vintage postcard with his name misspelled shows the monument that marks the spot in Atlanta where he was killed. The monument still exists but is in bad shape. He is buried in the family cemetery at Augusta College.

Four

PLACES TO VISIT AND REMEMBER

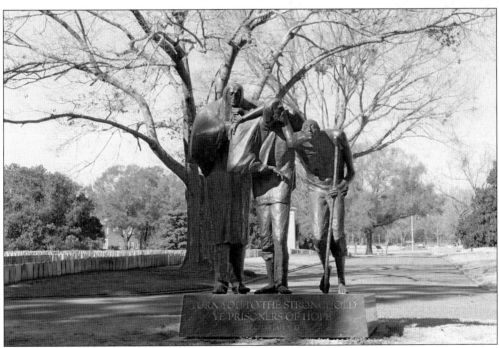

Anderson Station, as it was called at the time, was selected as a prison site in 1864, far from the fighting and near the end of the railroad line. Today, the Andersonville National Historic Site consists of the prison site "Camp Sumter," the National Prisoner of War Museum that honors prisoners of all wars, and the Andersonville National Cemetery. The Georgia Monument sculpted by W. J. Thompson honors all American prisoners of war. Nearby Andersonvlle features the Drummer Boy Museum, with artifacts and prison diorama, and the Wirz monument (see page 83).

the "BATTLE OF ATLANTA"

Exterior of Cyclorama, which houses the painting

ATLANTA, GEORGIA

(C) photos by Edgar Orr, Atlanta, Georgia

Atlanta features a number of places to visit and remember: Rhodes Hall, with its impressive Rise and Fall of the Confederacy stained-glass windows; Atlanta History Center with the DuBose Collection of artifacts; and the state capitol, with statuary and battle flags. The Atlanta Cyclorama and Civil War Museum is a can't-miss site. It houses the world's largest painting, *The Battle of Atlanta*, which is 50 feet by 400 feet, and through a presentation of commentary and music, visitors are brought back to the Battle of Atlanta in July 1864. The *Texas*, the locomotive that chased the *General* in reverse during the great locomotive chase, can be found in the lobby.

Confederate Monument, Unknown Dead, Oakland Cemetery, Atlanta, Ga

Buried in Atlanta's Oakland Cemetery are the remains of approximately 6,900 Confederate soldiers, and a large obelisk monument honors them. The first Confederate Memorial Service held there was on April 29, 1866. The monument to the "Unknown Confederate Dead" was sculpted by T. M. Brady of Canton on a design suggested by Col. John Milledge, based on the French monument Lion of Lucerne. Buried in Oakland are Gov. Joseph E. Brown, Captain Fuller, and Generals Avery, Evans, Gartrell, Gordon, Iverson, McKay, and W. S. Walker. Nearby Westview Cemetery features a Confederate monument surrounded by 347 Confederate veterans.

Built from scratch, the Augusta Powder Works began making gunpowder in 1862. It became the Confederacy's largest gunpowder manufacturing plant and in its time was the world's finest gunpowder facility. After the war, Col. George Rains, the man most responsible for its building, asked that the more than 150-foot chimney be spared as a monument to the Confederate dead. In addition, Georgia's finest county monument, dedicated to the men of Richmond County, can be found on Broad Street (see page 104). An older memorial marker can be found in front of St. James Church, and Georgia's oldest Confederate monument, dating to 1866, can be found at nearby Fort Gordon.

Augusta, Ga. The Old Powder Mill Chimney.
Monument to the Confederate Dead.

The Chickamauga and Chattanooga National Military Park Visitor Center, located near Fort Oglethorpe, Georgia, houses an interpretive center for the battles and houses the Fuller Gun Collection, a premier collection. The Chickamauga battlefield became the first national military park and was officially dedicated September 18–20, 1895. The park features over 1,400 monuments and historical markers. The Georgia monument serves as a tribute to the Georgians who fought in the Battle of Chickamauga. Atop the monument is a bronze Confederate standard bearer pointing northward. At the top of the base are figures honoring infantry, cavalry, and artillery.

First established as the Confederate Naval Museum in 1962, it was changed to Port Columbus for the grand opening of its new facility in March 2001. The museum features some of the rarest naval artifacts from the War Between the States and is the war's premier naval history site. It has over 40,000 square feet of exhibit space that includes an opportunity to go inside the interior of a replica Confederate ironclad. The museum houses the remnants of the ram CSS *Jackson* and gunboat CSS *Chattahoochee*. The museum looks at all aspects of the naval war: the blockade, blockade running, commerce raiders, river warfares, amphibious operation, technological innovations, and more. Former director of education Greg Startup gives a demonstration. (Courtesy of Port Columbus National Civil War Naval Museum)

An early postcard view of Liberty Hall shows the home of Alexander H. Stephens, vice president of the Confederacy and governor of Georgia. Today it is part of the A. H. Stephens State Historic Park. A Confederate museum housing one of the better collections of artifacts in Georgia is located adjacent to the house. Stephens was physically small and frail and resided here from 1834 until 1883, with the main house being rebuilt in 1875. He was arrested here at the end of the war and is buried next to the monument, erected in 1893. See page 2 for additional information.

Monument Erected to the
Confederate Cemetery at Marietta
near Atlanta, Ga.

The Marietta Confederate Cemetery was started in 1863 as a resting place for 20 Confederates killed in a train wreck. The monument dedicated in 1908 states, "To the 3,000 soldiers in this cemetery, from every southern state, who fell on Georgia soil, in defense of Georgia rights and Georgia homes." Nearby are Marietta's Kennesaw House, a historic hotel where the Andrews Raiders spent the night and that now serves as the Marietta Museum of History; the Kennesaw Mountain National Battlefield Park where 14 Georgia generals fought; and the Southern Museum of Civil War and Locomotive History that houses the *General*.

Sherman met great resistance from General Johnston's forces at New Hope Church in Dallas, Georgia, on May 25, 1864. Hoping to flank the Confederate Army, he sent troops towards Pickett's settlement. On May 27, the Battle of Pickett's Mill took place that resulted in a resounding defeat for the Federal troops, losing 1,600 men to the Confederates' 500. Today, the battlefield is part of the Pickett's Mill State Historic Site and is one of the best-preserved battlefields, having three walking trails and an interpretive museum center. (*Battlefields in Dixie Land*, W & A RR, 1928.)

Confederate Soldiers Graves, Savannah, Ga.

Savannah features a number of places to visit. Located at Laurel Grove Cemetery is the statue of Silence, which once adorned Savannah's original Confederate monument found in Forsyth Park. Buried in Laurel Grove Cemetery are Generals Francis S. Bartow, J. F. Gilmer, G. P. Harrison Sr., Peter A. S. McGlashen, L. McLaws, G. M. Sorrel, H. C. Wayne, and E. Willis. Bonaventure Cemetery, one of the South's most beautiful resting places, has the graves of Generals R. H. Anderson, H. R. Jackson, A. R. Lawton, H. W. Mercer, and C. C. Wilson and Cmdr. J. Tattnal III.

Along Georgia's coast are three coastal forts that defended Georgia in the War Between the States. Fort Pulaski National Monument, seen here after being bombarded by Federal forces, was built in 1847 with 25 million bricks and walls seven-and-a-half-feet thick. The use of rifled cannon marked the end of masonry fortifications, and it was here that the Immortal 600 were held at the end of the war. Fort Jackson was begun in 1808 and is Georgia's oldest brickwork fort. Fort McAllister State Park features an earthen works fort that overlooks the Ogeechee River, which saw eight naval battles.

The world's largest Confederate memorial is located at Stone Mountain, Georgia. Often referred to as the "Eighth Wonder of the World," the mountain is the largest exposed mass of granite in the world, standing over 780 feet above the surrounding terrain. Leased to the UDC in 1915, it was not until 1970 that the memorial was finished. The carving is 90 feet tall, 190 feet wide, and 400 feet above the ground. It features Pres. Jefferson Davis, Gen. Robert E. Lee, and Gen. Thomas J. "Stonewall" Jackson. For perspective, a cable car can be seen in the upper left of the image.

A vintage postcard image shows the home of Robert Toombs and can be toured today in Washington, Georgia. Toombs was Georgia's U.S. senator when the war started. Almost becoming the president of the Confederacy, he was appointed secretary of state but resigned the post to become a brigadier general. Toombs escaped capture after the war, living overseas, but he finally returned, an "unreconstructed rebel." He and his son-in-law, Gen. Dudley DuBose, are buried in Rest Haven Cemetery, Washington. The Washington Historical Museum has a collection of Confederate relics including a uniform of General Toombs. Washington was also the site of the last Confederate cabinet meeting, which is marked by a monument (see page 2).

INDEX

This index is not all-inclusive but is intended to assist the reader with major subjects. Most surnames are not listed with the exception of individuals that are featured.

RESOURCES AND RECOMMENDED READING

Avery, I. W. *The History of the State of Georgia, 1850–1881.* New York: Brown & Derby Publishers, 1881.

Bailey, Anne J. and Walter J. Fraser Jr. *Portraits of Conflict.* Fayetteville, AR: The University of Arkansas Press, 1996.

Barrow, Hugh W. *Private James R. Barrow and Company B Cobb's Legion Infantry.* Dalton, GA: self-published, 1996.

Century War Book. New York: The Century Co., 1894.

Cohen, Stan and James G. Bogle. *The General & The Texas.* Missoula, MT: Pictorial Histories Publishing Company, 1999.

Cunningham, S. A. *Confederate Veteran Magazine.* Nashville, TN: 1893–1932.

Derry, Joseph T. *Confederate Military History, Georgia.* Atlanta, GA: Confederate Publishing Company, 1899.

Evans, Lawton B. *A History of Georgia.* New York: American Book Company, 1898.

Georgia Division, United Daughters of the Confederacy. *Confederate Monuments and Markers in Georgia.* Fernandina Beach, FL: Wolfe Publishing, 2002.

Henderson, Lillian. *Roster of the Confederate Soldiers of Georgia.* Georgia Division, UDC, 1994.

Hubbell, Raynor. *Confederate Stamps, Old Letters, and History.* Griffin, GA: self-published, n.d.

Kerlin, Robert H. *Confederate Generals of Georgia.* Fayetteville, GA: Americana Historical Books, 1994.

Lenz, Richard J. *An Illustrated Travelers Guide—The Civil War in Georgia.* Watkinsville, GA: Infinity Press, 1995.

Lynch, John W. *The Dorman-Marshbourne Letters.* Senoia, GA: Down South Publishing Company, 1995.

McBryde, Randell W. *The Historic "General."* Chattanooga, TN: MacGowan & Cooke Co., 1904.

McKenney, Frank M. *The Standing Army.* Alpharetta, GA: W.H. Wolfe Associates, 1993.

Macon Telegraph. Macon, GA, 1912.

Roddy, Ray. *The Georgia Volunteer Infantry 1861–1865.* Kearney, NB: Morris Publishing, 1998.

Rogers, William Warren. *Thomas County During the Civil War.* Tallahassee, FL: Florida State University, 1964.

Rosenburg, R. B. *Living Monuments.* Chapel Hill, NC: University of North Carolina Press, 1993.

Sheppard, Peggy. *Andersonville, Georgia, U.S.A.* Leslie, GA: Sheppard Publications, 1973.

Smedlund, William S. *Camp Fires of Georgia's Troops 1861–1865.* Lithonia, GA: Kennesaw Mountain Press, 1995.

W & A RR. *Battlefields in Dixie Land.* Nashville, TN: self-published, 1928.